WOMEN'S ISSUES

THE
MAGILL
BIBLIOGRAPHIES

Other Magill Bibliographies:

The American Presidents—Norman S. Cohen
Black American Women Novelists—Craig Werner
Classical Greek and Roman Drama—Robert J. Forman
Contemporary Latin American Fiction—Keith H. Brower
Masters of Mystery and Detective Fiction—J. Randolph Cox
Nineteenth Century American Poetry—Philip K. Jason
Restoration Drama—Thomas J. Taylor
Twentieth Century European Short Story—Charles E. May
The Victorian Novel—Laurence W. Mazzeno

WOMEN'S ISSUES

An Annotated Bibliography

LAURA STEMPEL MUMFORD
Media Critic

SALEM PRESS
Pasadena, California   Englewood Cliffs, New Jersey

Library of Congress Cataloging-in-Publication Data

Mumford, Laura Stempel.
    Women's issues / Laura Stempel Mumford.
        p.   cm. — (Magill bibliographies)
    ISBN 0-89356-654-3
    1. Women—Bibliography.   2. Feminism—Bibli-
ography.   3. Women—United   States—Bibliography.
I. Title.   II. Series.
Z7961.M85   1989
[HQ1206]
016.30542 ' 0973—dc20   89-10831
                                             CIP

CONTENTS

EDITORIAL STAFF

ACKNOWLEDGMENTS

My first thanks are due to the librarians and others who have amassed wonderful collections of books on women in both the Madison Public Library and the Undergraduate Library of the University of Wisconsin-Madison. Thanks to those who have made it possible for me to keep thinking of myself as a feminist scholar and writer, particularly the women with whom I have read feminist theory. Special thanks to Sally Mitchell and Rima Apple, and to Bob Mumford, who put up with this project and more.

WOMEN'S ISSUES

INTRODUCTION

"Women's issues" can be defined in many ways. The most general definition would cover all topics of importance to women, but since most things that matter to women matter to men as well, the term needs to be narrowed further. More specifically, then, women's issues are those with special relevance to women's lives: the history and contributions of women as a group and as individuals; women's experiences with government, with the medical, scientific, and educational establishments, and with cultural institutions such as the media; women's economic position; physical aspects of women's experience (such as childbirth, sexuality, and life-cycle changes) and women's role in family life; crimes with predominantly female victims, such as rape and domestic violence; and movements—such as feminism—that seek to change women's lives. This bibliography focuses on how such issues affect the lives of individual women, members of particular groups, and women in general in the United States.

In the late twentieth century, shifts in women's status and changes in social structures such as the family have led to new questions about women's past, present, and future, and new research on women has grown up to address these topics. At the same time, the resurgence of the feminist movement in the 1960's and 1970's and the subsequent development of feminist scholarship have led to new kinds of writing on women and new ways to approach women's issues. In addition, many researchers and writers have responded to feminist scholarship, either by criticizing it or by drawing on its insights without becoming personally involved in the field of women's studies.

Although it is impossible to be perfectly comprehensive, this bibliography includes works by both women and men and from a variety of political, cultural, and social perspectives. Because of this variety, it is important for the reader to have a general sense of how different kinds of writers might address a particular topic.

The approach an individual writer takes can be affected by his or her gender, racial or ethnic identity, and sexual orientation. Because of their relative positions in American culture, for example, men and women may disagree in their analyses of social institutions such as government or religion. Similarly, their collective history in the United States and their experience as individuals may give women of color a different perspective on the family or the workplace; they may argue that white writers ignore the ways in which race or ethnicity affects those social structures. Lesbian writers may take issue with heterosexual writers' attitudes toward sexuality and maintain that such writers make assumptions that denigrate the lesbian experience. Such differences can also extend beyond immediate areas in which groups such as these have experienced dominance or discrimination. For instance, women of color may see women's experience as artists very differently from white women, and lesbians' approach to health-care issues may be significantly different from that of heterosexual women.

Political interests can also affect a writer's approach, and in the case of women's issues, that is particularly true when she or he has taken a feminist or antifeminist stance. A feminist perspective, for example, begins with the assumptions that women as a group have traditionally been discriminated against in economic, cultural, political, and personal spheres and that women's contributions to culture and society have been largely erased or overlooked. Feminist writers may disagree on the causes of discrimination or oppression, the extent to which it affects particular groups of women, and the possible solutions. Nevertheless, they agree that what has been seen as a universal view of the world is actually the view from which men see things and that, because conclusions drawn from men's experience are not necessarily applicable to women, women's voices must also be heard.

Similarly, an antifeminist perspective can affect the study of women's issues. Antifeminists and feminists share some ideas about women's position in society. For example, nearly everyone accepts statistics that demonstrate women's secondary status in the workplace, and almost no one disagrees about the existence of a pay differential between women and men. But feminists and antifeminists do disagree about why differences between women and men exist, whether such differences are positive or negative, and what, if anything, should be done about them.

In general, antifeminist writers tend to see as inevitable or desirable many of the things that feminists want to change, and their research is informed by these opinions. In fact, the difference between feminist and antifeminist studies often lies in the interpretation of information, rather than in the facts themselves. For example, where a feminist writer might interpret statistics on women's status in the workplace as evidence that they are discriminated against in training, hiring, and promotion, an antifeminist writer might use the same data to argue that women choose not to enter traditional male jobs and prefer to do the kind of work one usually associates with women or that they put their energies into childrearing and other family concerns and have less interest in careers. Some research also focuses on what are perceived as the negative effects of the women's movement, with writers arguing, for example, that recent changes in divorce laws, affirmative action policies, and family structures have worsened women's status rather than improved it.

This is simply a broad outline of some of the differences that can affect the approaches writers and researchers take. Because of them, most sections of this bibliography cite works that directly contradict one another, or that present completely different interpretations of very similar information. It is important to remember that the subjects addressed here are not easily resolved into "right" and "wrong" answers. While individual writers come to very different conclusions, all the works cited represent serious attempts to analyze and understand complex subjects.

The bibliography is divided into sections that deal with a single area or a group of related subjects, but this division by topic is far from rigid, and many of the subjects overlap. Some works appear in more than one section, and some citations describe subjects that are relevant to several categories. This reflects the overlap that occurs in real women's lives and experiences, where concerns about, for example, family and work cannot be entirely separated. The reader should keep this in mind when using this book.

A short list of sources that deal with women's issues in a general way is included at the end of this introduction. The works in this list should provide a broad context for the other sections and an introduction to women's status in the United States and around the world. Here and elsewhere, there will be citations for books and essays that include extensive bibliographies and resource lists which will point to other sources and to related subjects.

The next section, "History, Politics, and Education," focuses on the history of women in the United States. Women have always made important contributions to the development of society and culture, although that participation has not always been acknowledged. Since the late 1960's, scholars working specifically on the experiences of women have added much to the traditional view of history as the story of men's accomplishments, and this section includes many works by these writers. Several related topics are also included in this section: women in government and politics, the development of education for women (including several works on women's studies as an academic field), and biographies and autobiographies of women who have had an impact on history. This last subsection also includes some diaries and other autobiographical writings by "ordinary" women— women who are not famous, but whose reflections on life illuminate some aspect of women's condition.

Although the term "feminism" only came into use at the turn of the century, many of the ideas associated with that word go back to at least the late eighteenth century. "The Women's Movement" deals with the U.S. movement from its origins in the mid-nineteenth century, when it was closely associated with the abolition movement; the development of contemporary feminism, including the campaign for the Equal Rights Amendment (ERA); and issues of sexuality and racism raised by lesbians and women of color in contemporary feminism. (More entries on race and ethnicity and on lesbian experience will be found throughout the bibliography.) This section includes not only histories of the movement but also examples of feminist theory and critiques of feminism by both participants and opponents.

The citations in "Economics" deal with women in the workplace and the economy, and with women's experience of poverty. Subjects include women's choices about work, and experiences in the work force, sexual discrimination, sexual harassment, and labor organizing. These citations should provide a context in which to consider issues related to women workers and career women, as well as those women who are homeless, on welfare, or unemployed.

"Health Issues and Sexuality" covers a wide range of subjects related to women's health and includes categories on sexuality and reproduction. In this context, the term "sexuality" refers to questions of sexual identity and behavior, with considerations of both heterosexual and lesbian women. Reproductive issues include birth control, abortion, pregnancy, and childbirth, as well as the newer areas of infertility and reproductive technology. The final subsection covers a variety of health-related topics, such as anorexia nervosa and other eating disorders, menstruation and menopause, and women and Acquired Immune Deficiency Syndrome (AIDS). Many of the issues treated in "Health Issues and Sexuality" are extremely controversial, and both technological developments and public opinion change rapidly. It is difficult for a bibliography to be completely up-to-date, but the works cited here should provide basic information through 1988.

"Family, Home, and Relationships" addresses marriage, divorce, and related subjects. Nontraditional families, childrearing, how children learn sex roles, and policy issues such as day-care provisions and parental leave are some of the topics included. Because of their importance in family life, this section also covers motherhood—both women's experiences as mothers and cultural definitions of mothering—and domesticity, which includes housework, images of home and homemaking, and such questions as how technology affects people's ideas about those things.

Many of the topics already described, such as sexuality, reappear in the section entitled "Psychology." This section examines both traditional psychological theories about women (from Sigmund Freud and Carl Gustav Jung to more recent writers) and feminist critiques of them. An array of approaches to psychology is included, as well as a variety of alternatives to them. (Please note that there is considerable overlap between this section and the category of sex roles in the section "Family, Home, and Relationships.")

"Violence Against Women" covers forms of violence that particularly affect women: rape and domestic violence (or spouse and child abuse, including incest). Because much of the current debate over pornography centers on its possible relationship to violence against women, this issue has also been included here. The citations on pornography include both writers who believe that it is closely linked to violence and writers who disagree and who oppose its censorship.

Included in the section "Religion and Spirituality" are works dealing with women's position in traditional religions—particularly Christianity and Judaism— and women's responses to them, as well as material on the recent interest among some women in ancient religions and goddess worship. This section includes writings by women who have chosen to stay within traditional organized religions as well as writings by those who have chosen other ways—especially a return to ancient traditions of worship and witchcraft—to fulfill their spiritual needs.

The final section, "Women and the Arts," considers women's participation in the arts and artistic renditions of women and their experiences. It covers the visual arts, literature, music, and popular media such as film and television and includes both histories and biographies of women involved in traditional artistic movements and women's responses to and critiques of those traditions.

This bibliography is intended for high school and college students, and every effort has been made to include only those works that can be found in a good public or college library. Few libraries will contain every single work cited here, but all of the works should be available through an inter-library loan program or a bookstore. Many of the entries list both the original publications (likely to be found in libraries) and information on more accessible reprints (likely to be found in bookstores).

Because the intended audience for these entries will vary in ability, background, and interest, the citations vary as well. While many of the listings contain scholarly, historical, or theoretical works, biographies and personal narratives have also been included throughout the bibliography. This kind of writing can make a complex subject more accessible by giving readers some insight into how individuals grappled with it; if a reader has difficulty with the more theoretical analyses, it might be helpful to begin with a personal account. Books and essays that are not explicitly identified as autobiographical may also include personal reminiscences, and many works make use of personal accounts, case histories, and anecdotes. In addition, when individual essays in collections or anthologies are cited, readers might find other, uncited parts of those books equally interesting.

The sources described here range from popular works written for a general audience to specialized treatments of topics. The books and essays cited vary in their level of difficulty, and some make extremely sophisticated theoretical or academic arguments or demand some familiarity with the topic. Even the most difficult ones, however, are accessible to college juniors and seniors. The citations should make it clear which works are introductory, or survey the field, and which are aimed at more experienced readers. Some of the books described are actually intended as handbooks or popular guides, and these can provide excellent introductions to a complex subject. Do not be put off because a title suggests that a handbook is meant for readers with a personal involvement in the topic. Those that are listed here are written for a general audience and may be the best way for a reader unfamiliar with an issue to begin researching it. (Although none of the works listed is a textbook, many are appropriate for classroom use, and teachers should find the anthologies and essay collections extremely useful.)

Where books include illustrations, figures, tables, or particularly helpful resource lists or bibliographies, those have been mentioned. Although most of the books have indexes and reference lists, those noted in the citations are usually particularly helpful or specialized ones—for example, a comprehensive bibliography, an index of names, or an unusual classified list—or appear in works where you might not expect an index (such as in essay collections). Most of the scholarly and historical studies also include notes or other source citations, and those have only been mentioned if they are unusual or highly specialized.

The best way to begin using this bibliography is to choose a section and read through all the citations in it. This will provide a sense of the major issues, the kinds of positions writers have taken on them, and the range of materials available. If none of the works seems appropriate, seek out the ones whose citations mention introductions to the subject, useful resource lists, or extensive bibliographies. These will provide a more detailed explanation of the important questions and problems or will lead to sources not included here. Also consider looking in anthologies and collections, especially those whose contents seem to cover a wide range of subjects. The introductory and bibliographic material in such books can often be very helpful.

In researching a particular topic, be sure to check in related sections for additional readings. For example, if women's sexual behavior is the subject, you should be sure to look at all the citations in the section "Health Issues and Sexuality," particularly those on topics related to reproduction, as well as citations in "The Women's Movement," "Psychology," and "Religion and Spirituality," all of which include writings on sexuality. If the subject is women and work, begin with "Economics" but also try "Women and the Arts" (for ideas about how women artists work), "Family, Home, and Relationships" (for information about how women make decisions about career and family life), and even "Health Issues and Sexuality" (for materials on work-related health problems). The sections "History, Politics, and Education" and "The Women's Movement" are always worth considering, since many of the works cited in them discuss how issues raised in other sections have been considered in the past and how participants in various aspects of the women's movement have seen them.

One word of warning in using this bibliography: Although the entries listed here cover a wide range of issues, they by no means exhaust the writings—or even the topics—available. The books and essays included are not meant to be complete lists of available work on any one subject, but merely to point readers and students in the right direction. That is why the presence of resource and bibliographic lists has been emphasized. In addition, many interesting subjects—women in the performing arts, for example, and women and science—have been omitted as individual categories, although there are references to them in entries for other topics. Others (such as women and sports) are relatively new areas for scholars dealing with women's issues; thus, the body of work available is smaller than that on many other topics, and much of the serious research is still at a specialized level.

General Studies

Bernard, Jessie. *The Female World*. New York: Free Press, 1981.
> Massive analysis of what Bernard claims is the largely unexplored single-sex world of women; she argues that women and men are socially and culturally segregated, and she considers the history of the separate spheres. Explores marriage and kinship relations, social class, economy, language, and other cultural issues among women living in the "male" world and in communities of women (such as convents), emphasizing the positive aspects of the "female" world. Massive bibliography. Name and subject indexes.

Bianchi, Suzanne M., and Daphne Spain. *American Women in Transition*. New York: Russell Sage Foundation, 1986.

Using data from the census of 1980, authors discuss changes in American women's lives since 1960 and interpret statistics in the light of social science research. Sections cover marriage patterns, childbearing, living arrangements, education, participation in the work force, poverty, and tensions between work and home. Argues that cultural changes—attitudes, provision of day care, and so on—have lagged behind the reality of women's lives. Includes tables, figures, a bibliography, and an index.

Clark, Judith Freeman. *Almanac of American Women in the Twentieth Century*. Englewood Cliffs, N.J.: Prentice-Hall, 1987.
Short essays introduce decade-by-decade chapters recounting important events for women. Categories include political issues, education, popular culture, labor, science, the military, and sports. Features short biographies of important women, many with photographs. Index.

Gibson, Anne, and Timothy Fast. *The Women's Atlas of the United States*. New York: Facts on File, 1986.
Maps illustrate statistics about American women, including education, employment, family, health, crime, and politics. Data are summarized in charts and section introductions. Bibliography and index.

James, Edward J., Janet Wilson James, and Paul S. Boyer, eds. *Notable American Women, 1607-1950*. 3 vols. Cambridge, Mass.: Harvard University Press, 1971.
The standard reference for information on well-known American women. Lengthy biographical entries on a wide range of notable women in a variety of fields. Each entry includes references. Classified index groups subjects by profession (abolitionists, educators, writers, and the like).

Morgan, Robin, ed. *Sisterhood Is Global: The International Women's Movement Anthology*. Garden City, N.Y.: Anchor Press/Doubleday, 1984.
Almanac of women around the world, emphasizing a feminist perspective on international women's experience. More than sixty countries represented, with summaries of women's economic and social positions through history and individual essays about feminist movements. Includes a comprehensive introduction, useful statistics, a lengthy bibliography, and a glossary of relevant terms.

Newland, Kathleen. *The Sisterhood of Man*. New York: W. W. Norton, 1979.
Introduction to the social, economic, and cultural status of women around the world, with cross-cultural discussions of a wide range of topics. Individual chapters treat women's legal position, politics, education, health, work, family, and images of women in mass media. Conclusion asserts that, while women's status has changed, traditional notions of appropriate roles combine with

women's continued isolation from political power, literacy, and economic independence to perpetuate their secondary position. Tables, figures. Selected readings organized by topic.

Partnow, Elaine, ed. *The Quotable Woman, 1800-On*. Garden City, N.Y.: Anchor Press/Doubleday, 1978.
Encyclopedia of quotations from an international array of women—as diverse as actress Marie Dressler, playwright Lorraine Hansberry, and designer Coco Chanel—on a variety of topics. The collection is intended to redress the shortage of women in standard encyclopedias of quotations. Entries are organized in chronological order, and all quotations cite sources. Biographical and subject indexes.

Seager, Joni, and Ann Olson. *Women in the World: An International Atlas*. New York: Simon & Schuster, 1986.
Colorful maps describe women's status around the world. Includes statistics on legal rights, marriage, health, violence, contraception and abortion, population policies, media, and women's role in the labor force. One useful table summarizes data by country; another section gives definitions and explains standards used in maps. Bibliography and index.

Sicherman, Barbara, and Carol Hurd Green, eds. *Notable American Women: The Modern Period*. Cambridge, Mass.: Harvard University Press, 1980.
Supplement to *Notable American Women, 1607-1950*. Updates the original biographical dictionary, covering the period from 1950 to the mid-1970's.

Uglow, Jennifer, ed. *The International Dictionary of Women's Biography*. New York: Continuum, 1982.
Dictionary of international women scholars, artists, scientists, activists, criminals, athletes, and others. A wide-ranging collection of historical and contemporary figures (as disparate as poet Anne Sexton and country singer Tammy Wynette) chosen for their impact on women's lives or for their "legendary" status. Subject index by categories (public life, cultural life, physical achievements, and "colorful characters"). Illustrations and guide to other references.

Woloch, Nancy. *Women and the American Experience*. New York: Alfred A. Knopf, 1984.
Survey of American women from Colonial times to the present. Woloch pairs two kinds of chapters, alternating "episodes"—discussions of individual women or events—with more general syntheses of historical periods. Includes substantial lists of suggested readings for each pair of chapters, illustrations and photographs, and considerable discussion of black women's experience.

HISTORY, POLITICS, AND EDUCATION

Women in History

Aptheker, Bettina. *Woman's Legacy: Essays on Race, Sex, and Class in American History*. Amherst: University of Massachusetts Press, 1982.
Essays focusing on racial issues in women's experience in American history, covering topics such as women's role in the abolition movement, connections between the suffrage movement and antilynching campaigns, black women in the professions, and W. E. B. Du Bois' theories on women. "The Matriarchal Mirage: The Moynihan Connection Historical Perspective" explores the origins in post-World War II social conditions of the controversial myth (popularized by Daniel Patrick Moynihan) that black women are emasculating matriarchs. Index.

Armitage, Susan, and Elizabeth Jameson, eds. *The Women's West*. Norman: University of Oklahoma Press, 1987.
Collection of essays on women's role in the American West. Contributors analyze images of women in the visual arts and literature of the West; the role of women in the fur trade and mining towns; women as homesteaders, prostitutes, mothers, and workers; and women in politics, including the suffrage movement. Essays present women as active agents rather than passive "ladies" and treat class issues, race and ethnicity (including several considerations of Native American women), and how women's experiences in the West changed idealized sex roles. Illustrations. Index.

Beard, Mary Ritter. *Woman as Force in History: A Study in Traditions and Realities*. New York: Macmillan, 1946. Reprint. New York: Collier Books, 1962.
Classic early work of women's history. Beard examines women's role from prehistory to modern times and the development of the idea that legal equity is the solution to women's secondary status. Argues that women have made important contributions—promoting civilization over barbarism—but that these have been overlooked by traditional historians. Includes lengthy bibliography.

Bell, Susan Groag, and Karen M. Offen, eds. *Women, the Family, and Freedom: The Debate in Documents*. 2 vols. Stanford, Calif.: Stanford University Press, 1983.
This huge collection of essays, speeches, legal briefs, fictional excerpts, and other writings traces the arguments in Western countries over women, their position in and relationship to the family, and their social and political rights, from 1750 to 1950. Selections are by both male and female writers (including famous and less well-known women) and are grouped by historical periods.

Within each period, selections are divided into sections on topics such as men's authority in marriage, women's political consciousness, controversies over women's education, suffrage, and psychology. Editors provide a general introduction to the entire collection, introductions to each historical section, and headnotes for individual topics and documents. Suggested reading list, bibliography, and index provided for each volume.

Boxer, Marilyn J., and Jean H. Quataert, eds. *Connecting Spheres: Women in the Western World, 1500 to the Present.* Foreword by Joan W. Scott. New York: Oxford University Press, 1987.
Collection of scholarly essays grouped by historical era—1500 to 1750, 1750 to 1890, and 1890 to the present. Each section begins with an editors' essay providing a historical overview of the period. Individual essays address marriage, economy, religion, science, domesticity, feminism, politics, and war, each one introduced by an abstract and including suggestions for further reading. Specific topics range from Sarah Hanley's "Family and State in Early Modern France: The Marriage Pact" to Maria-Barbara Watson-Franke's " 'I Am Somebody!' Women's Changing Sense of Self in the German Democratic Republic." Figures, tables, illustrations. Index.

Bridenthal, Renate, and Claudia Koonz, eds. *Becoming Visible: Women in European History.* Boston: Houghton Mifflin, 1977. Rev. ed., with Susan Mosher Stuard, 1987.
Influential collection of essays on women's history. Includes analyses of early egalitarian societies, the classical and medieval periods, witchcraft, preindustrial capitalism, and women's roles in the Russian Revolution and Nazi Germany. Includes Joan Kelly-Gadol's landmark essay, "Did Women Have a Renaissance?" focusing on courtly love to argue that traditional notions of historical periods often have no relevance to women's experience. With an introduction and an index.

Brown, Dorothy. *Setting a Course: American Women in the 1920s.* In *American Women in the Twentieth Century*, edited by Barbara Haber. Boston: Twayne/ G. K. Hall, 1987.
Examines a decade characterized by major and rapid changes in political and cultural institutions, including women's first opportunity to vote. Brown focuses on how the "New Woman" of the 1920's dealt with new options and discusses political reform, work, education, religion, family life, and literature. Short bibliographic essay. (This series includes volumes on the 1930's, 1940's, and 1950's, with studies forthcoming on the 1960's, 1970's, and the period from 1900 to 1920.)

Brumberg, Joan Jacobs. *Fasting Girls: The Emergence of Anorexia Nervosa as a Modern Disease.* Cambridge, Mass.: Harvard University Press, 1988.

Important study of anorexia, centering on nineteenth and twentieth century attempts to understand eating disorders. Although focusing on a single disease, Brumberg also examines historical attitudes toward food, family life, female adolescence, notions of illness and wellness, and female sexuality, and illuminates the development of contemporary medical theories about women's behavior. Illustrations.

Bullough, Vern L., Brenda Shelton, and Sarah Slavin. *The Subordinated Sex: A History of Attitudes Toward Women*. Rev. ed. Athens: University of Georgia Press, 1988.
The authors trace the history of ideas about women, beginning with the basis of Western attitudes in ancient cultures and concluding with the contemporary United States. Includes chapters on women and Christianity, American attitudes from the Colonial period on, and cross-cultural considerations, including women in Islam, China, and India. Discusses and analyzes a variety of perspectives—both supportive and denigrating of women—including proposed solutions and challenges to women's marginal or secondary status, and emphasizing the cross-cultural and historical nature of that position.

Carroll, Berenice A., ed. *Liberating Women's History: Theoretical and Critical Essays*. Urbana: University of Illinois Press, 1976.
Collection of essays on women's history, including critiques of the writing of American history and theoretical arguments about how women's history should be constructed. Essays cover a variety of topics, from seventeenth century English gynecology to Mexican convents, and include work by prominent historians of women—among them Ann J. Lane, Linda Gordon, Gerda Lerner, Sarah Pomeroy, Alice Kessler-Harris.

Culley, Margo, ed. *A Day at a Time: The Diary Literature of American Women from 1764 to the Present*. New York: Feminist Press at the City University of New York, 1985.
Selections from diaries of "ordinary" American women representing different periods and ways of life. The book also traces the changing form and function of the diary from a semipublic social and family history to a forum for private self-examination. Entries discuss war, family, work, migration and immigration, and politics. Includes an introduction and a bibliography.

Ewen, Elizabeth. *Immigrant Women in the Land of Dollars: Life and Culture on the Lower East Side, 1890-1925*. New York: Monthly Review Press, 1985.
Study of the experience of immigrant women on New York City's Lower East Side, drawing on autobiographies, letters, fiction, oral history, and contemporary observations (by social workers and others) to emphasize the women's

own perspectives. Ewen makes extensive use of detail about individual women in order to draw a larger picture of how immigrant women from various European countries coped with American life and society. Chapters address the Old World, the actual immigration experience, work (including organized labor and the women's participation in labor unions and strikes), health, homes, money and economic situations, and urban life. Illustrations.

Fox-Genovese, Elizabeth. *Within the Plantation Household: Black and White Women of the Old South.* Chapel Hill: University of North Carolina Press, 1988.
A history of the experience of black slave women and white slave-owning women in the antebellum South. Fox-Genovese departs from many other feminist historians in arguing that slave-owning women had too great an investment in their privileges to be "closet" feminists or to support abolition, and that only black women were genuine abolitionists. She also insists that the institution of slavery made it impossible for black and white women to form any kind of "sisterly" bonds. Draws extensively on the writings—both published and unpublished—of white women like Mary Boykin Chestnut and of black women like Harriet Jacobs, using personal and imaginative writing to explore notions of "ladylike" behavior, women's rights, and attitudes toward slavery, family, sexuality and sexual abuse, the Civil War, and other subjects. Illustrations. Lengthy bibliography.

Fraser, Antonia. *The Weaker Vessel.* New York: Alfred A. Knopf, 1984. Reprint. New York: Vintage Books, 1985.
An anecdotal history of women in seventeenth century England, with an emphasis on women's own voices as expressed through their letters, diaries, and other sources. Fraser questions whether women were as "weak" in real life as law, theology, and philosophy insisted. Sections address marriage (including relationships between husbands and wives, the experience of widowhood); the impact of the Civil Wars (1642-1651), including women's role in war; and the Restoration of the monarchy (1651). Individual chapters deal with midwives, actresses, writers, and women as religious leaders. Epilogue describes women as "strong vessels where they had the opportunity." Includes useful chronology of important events from 1603 (the death of Elizabeth I) to 1702. Illustrations.

Friedman, Jean E., and William G. Shade, eds. *Our American Sisters: Women in American Life and Thought.* Boston: Allyn & Bacon, 1973, 2d ed. 1976.
Essays on gender issues from the Puritans to the present. Sections deal with Colonial America (sexuality, women's role in public life, religious activism, and interracial relationships), the Victorian era (changes in economic and social status, slave families, working-class women at home and work), the Pro-

gressive Era (feminism and the trade union movement, love and marriage, the "New Woman" in the South), and the twentieth century (popular film, the sexual revolution, black women, and feminism). Contributors include historians Linda Kerber, Gerda Lerner, William O'Neill, Anne Firor Scott, and Jill Conway.

Giddings, Paula. *When and Where I Enter: The Impact of Black Women on Race and Sex in America*. New York: William Morrow, 1984.
History of black women in the United States from slavery to the present, with particular emphasis on political activism. Includes chapters on black women's efforts to develop a new identity after abolition, antilynching campaigns of the late nineteenth century, the rise of black colleges, the impact of the Depression and World War II, and the importance of black and feminist organizing before World War I and in the 1960's and 1970's.

Hartman, Mary, and Lois W. Banner, eds. *Clio's Consciousness Raised: New Perspectives on the History of Women*. New York: Harper & Row, 1974.
An early collection of essays by prominent historians of women, among them Ann Douglas Wood, Carroll Smith-Rosenberg, Linda Gordon, Judith R. Walkowitz, and Daniel Walkowitz. Contributors address subjects such as nineteenth century notions of women's health, origins of the birth-control movement, medieval European families, Victorian feminism, religion in America, and prostitution.

Kaledin, Eugenia. *Mothers and More: American Women in the 1950s*. In *American Women in the Twentieth Century*, edited by Barbara Haber. Boston: Twayne/ G. K. Hall, 1984.
A history of women's experience during the decade usually characterized in terms of their victimization by myths of suburban motherhood. Kaledin argues that women in the 1950's were not merely victims but were often genuinely satisfied because they cherished a sense of "separate but equal" spheres. She also emphasizes women's creative achievements in the arts, describing many of the decade's most successful women as "gifted outsiders." Chapters address education, work, women, and politics (including considerable discussion of Eleanor Roosevelt), women writers and artists, black women, and health issues. Bibliographic essay. Illustrations, figures.

Kerber, Linda. *Women of the Republic: Intellect and Ideology in Revolutionary America*. Chapel Hill: University of North Carolina Press, 1980.
Using documents such as diaries, letters, and legal records, Kerber examines women's role in the revolutionary period. She argues that despite men's assumption that women were outside the political community, women were deeply affected by both the war and the development of the new republic.

Describes the evolution of new laws and the notion of "Republican Motherhood," mothers as guardians and nurturers of civic virtue.

Labarge, Margaret Wade. *A Small Sound of the Trumpet: Women in Medieval Life.*
Boston: Beacon Press, 1986.
A history of medieval women, focusing on Europe from 1100 to 1500. Labarge
discusses women as queens, noblewomen, women in religious life (including
nuns and mystics), women workers, healers, and "women on the fringe"
(criminals, prostitutes, heretics, sorcerers, and so on, including Joan of Arc).
Individual chapters consider a wide range of women's contributions to medieval culture as writers, artists (defined to include traditional crafts like embroidery), and founders of religious houses. Labarge draws on surviving records,
manuscripts, and works of art and literature, and largely because of the sources
available, pays much attention to the experience and contributions of exceptional individual women like writer Christine de Pisan. Introduction and chapter on "The Precursors" provide historical context; "The Mould for Medieval
Women" describes medieval thought on women's role, health, and social and
legal status. Illustrations, including many examples of work by medieval artists. Recommended list for further reading.

Lerner, Gerda. *The Creation of Patriarchy.* New York: Oxford University Press,
1986.
Controversial examination of patriarchy's origins by a prominent feminist historian. Lerner argues that men's appropriation of women's reproductive capacity represents the first form of "private property" and the beginning of
women's oppression. She includes extensive discussion of goddess worship and
pre-classical cultures, but critics argue that Lerner's use of classical and other
sources is faulty. Appendix of definitions for basic terms useful in women's
history. Bibliography.

—————————, ed. *Black Women in White America: A Documentary History.* New
York: Random House, 1973. Reprint. New York: Vintage Books, 1973.
Collection of documents relevant to the experiences of black women in the
United States from 1811 to the 1970's. Includes writings by and about black
women on slavery, resistance, education, work, racism, and politics. Introduc-
tions to each section and brief explanations of organizations and sources.
Bibliographical notes.

Morello, Karen Berger. *The Invisible Bar: The Woman Lawyer in America, 1638 to
the Present.* New York: Random House, 1986.
The first complete history of U.S. women lawyers, including chapters on
women as lawyers, law students, and judges and separate chapters on black
women lawyers, Ivy League law schools, and major law firms. Morello, a

lawyer who conducted hundreds of interviews for the book, argues that women lawyers have continually been invisible—even to one another—and despite recent outward improvements, such as the appointment of Sandra Day O'Connor to the U.S. Supreme Court, their status has not changed substantially. She sees the majority of women lawyers as still relegated to the "second tier," accorded less prestige, and kept from the influential circles of banking, finance, and high-level politics to which men have access. Illustrations.

Rowbotham, Sheila. *Hidden from History: Rediscovering Women in History from the Seventeenth Century to the Present.* London: Pluto Press, 1973. Reprint. New York: Vintage Books, 1976.
A survey of English women's history from a Marxist-feminist perspective. Rowbotham focuses on ways in which women's contributions have been overlooked and emphasizes ties between women and the trade-union movement. The American edition includes an introduction useful for readers unfamiliar with English history.

Ryan, Mary P. *Womanhood in America: From Colonial Times to the Present.* 3d ed. New York: Franklin Watts, 1983.
Study traces ideas about gender, particularly the notion of "womanhood," in U.S. history. Ryan outlines three major stages: the seventeenth century patriarchal household economy, the subsequent philosophy of "separate spheres" (associating women with private, men with public concerns), and the greater integration that occurred in the twentieth century. She demonstrates how both "womanhood" and the larger gender system adapt to social changes and cultural diversity, although she also argues that the contemporary women's movement provides a fundamental challenge to both. Chapters treat the rise of industrial capitalism, immigrants, women in reform movements, culture before and after World War II, and the impact of feminism.

Smith-Rosenberg, Carroll. *Disorderly Conduct: Visions of Gender in Victorian America.* New York: Alfred A. Knopf, 1985.
Essays on gender in nineteenth century America, covering topics such as the life cycle, hysteria, pornography, and abortion. "Hearing Women's Words: A Feminist Reconstruction of History" reviews the development of feminist study of women's history. The collection includes Smith-Rosenberg's most famous essay, "The Female World of Love and Ritual," which argues that nineteenth century American women and men led sex-segregated lives, with women friends and relatives providing one another with practical and emotional support.

Sterling, Dorothy, ed. *We Are Your Sisters: Black Women in the Nineteenth Century.* New York: W. W. Norton, 1984.

Original documents concerning black women's experience from 1800 to the 1880's, including excerpts from interviews, letters, diaries, autobiographies, and newspaper articles. The book makes extensive use of oral history, retains original language and spelling, and covers a wide social range—from uneducated laborers to teachers and professional writers. Entries examine life under slavery and freedom before, during, and after the Civil War—in both the North and the South—and deal with family life, work, violence, and education. With illustrations, a selected bibliography, and an index.

Ulrich, Laurel Thatcher. *Good Wives: Image and Reality in the Lives of Women in Northern New England, 1650-1750*. New York: Alfred A. Knopf, 1982.
This study of the early Colonies uses individual women's experiences to draw larger pictures of women's lives, including both the images (often biblical) by which they were understood and the often quite different daily reality. Women are discussed in their roles as wives, neighbors, mothers (including details on childbearing and related health issues), housekeepers, church members, workers, and transgressors of the moral and social code through sexual and other behavior. A chapter on women captured during the Indian Wars emphasizes how captivity tales were shaped by racism. Concludes with notion of "heroines"—women who, in times of crisis, took normal or acceptable behavior to extremes, becoming either saints or "viragos." Illustrations, including historical maps. Bibliographic essay.

Weatherford, Doris. *Foreign and Female: Immigrant Women in America, 1840-1930*. New York: Schocken Books, 1986.
A study including all major European immigrant groups of the period and women in both urban and rural America. Individual chapters consider health, reproduction, death, religion, morality (including marriage and divorce), domesticity, work, the effects on the women of separation from their origins and homelands, family, their views of the New World, and immigrant women's contributions to the United States. Illustrations. Bibliography.

Weinberg, Sydney Stahl. *The World of Our Mothers: The Lives of Jewish Immigrant Women*. Chapel Hill: University of North Carolina Press, 1988.
Study of the experiences of East European Jewish women immigrating to the United States from the 1890's to the 1920's, based on extensive interviews with forty-six immigrants. Includes chapters on life in Europe, but focuses on education, family life, work, religion, cultural identity, assimilation, and other aspects of the American experience. Illustrations. Glossary of Yiddish terms. Bibliography.

White, Deborah Gray. *Ain't I a Woman? Female Slaves in the Plantation South*. New York: W. W. Norton, 1985.
Study of the experiences of black women slaves in the American South. White

argues that their position was essentially an extreme version of women's position in general—which affected even those women active in the struggles for abolition and women's rights—but that black women's lives were circumscribed by race and the class distinctions implicit in the institution of slavery. She begins with an examination of cultural stereotypes of black women, such as Jezebel (the sexually active and therefore exploitable women) and Mammy (the idealized selfless mother), considering how they drew on other archetypes of women's behavior. Individual chapters discuss the nature of female slavery (including sexual abuse), experiences across the life cycle, the network existing among female slaves, and the aftermath of slavery. Selected bibliography includes unpublished manuscript collections.

Women in Government and Politics

Abzug, Bella, with Mim Kelber. *The Gender Gap: Bella Abzug's Guide to Political Power for American Women*. Boston: Houghton Mifflin, 1984.
The former New York congresswoman analyzes the "gender gap"—the difference between men's and women's voting patterns—with a focus on women in American political life in the 1970's and 1980's. Includes discussion of the ERA campaign, fights for equality within the Democratic and Republican parties, the importance of women's vote in the 1980 election, and women candidates. Abzug advocates "mobilizing the majority" (women) to change the national political agenda. Appendix lists directory of "organizations active in gender-gap politics."

Baxter, Sandra, and Marjorie Lansing. *Women and Politics: The Visible Majority*. Ann Arbor: University of Michigan Press, 1983.
Analysis of women's participation in the American political process—including considerations of the gender gap, women's attitudes toward public policy, and women's roles in grass-roots and national political organizations. Includes a chapter of cross-cultural comparisons and two chapters on black women voters. Argues that, while it is too early to know exactly what impact their vote will have, women now constitute a coherent group that will work for human rights. Tables. Bibliography.

Carroll, Susan J. *Women as Candidates in American Politics*. Bloomington: Indiana University Press, 1985.
Study based on a questionnaire distributed to all women candidates for state political office in the 1976 primaries and general elections. Carroll argues that women are underrepresented at all levels of elective office and that better access to financing, additional experience, and traditional incumbency gives male candidates considerable advantages. Tables. Appendices describe data collection, questionnaire.

Chamberlin, Hope. *A Minority of Members: Women in the U.S. Congress*. New York: Praeger, 1973.

Chronologically arranged biographical essays on the first eighty women elected to Congress, from Jeannette Rankin (Republican from Montana)—elected to the House in 1916, four years before women got the national vote, and the only member to vote against U.S. entry into both world wars—to Patricia Schroeder (Democrat from Colorado), elected in 1972. Brief general introduction and an introduction to each chronological grouping. Essays trace changing attitudes toward women in office. Illustrations. Alphabetical list.

Chisholm, Shirley. *The Good Fight*. New York: Harper & Row, 1973.

Chisholm, the first woman and first black candidate for President of the United States in a major party, analyzes her 1972 Democratic campaign from the primaries to the national convention. Includes discussions of her own failures and those of nominee George McGovern (who, she argues, failed to mobilize women and minorities effectively) and her career as a congresswoman. Appendices reprint position papers and campaign speeches.

Cook, Blanche Weisen, ed. *Crystal Eastman on Women and Revolution*. New York: Oxford University Press, 1978.

Selected writings by an early twentieth century political activist who participated in both the American and British feminist, Socialist, and pacifist movements. The collection covers all of Eastman's political interests, but newspaper articles and essays specifically focusing on women look at love and marriage, birth control, fashion, protective legislation, suffrage, and women's international political movements. Index.

Dworkin, Andrea. *Right-Wing Women*. New York: Perigee Books, 1983.

A prominent radical feminist (most famous as an antipornography activist) examines women's reasons for joining conservative political movements, especially those associated with right-wing political activism. Dworkin argues that such women actually share some insights with feminists, recognize their own secondary position in society, and see the traditional family structures, conservative values, fundamentalist religion, and other right-wing goals as the only effective way to gain protection. Includes analysis of antifeminism, which Dworkin describes as a basic tool for persuading conservative women that gender inequalities are inevitable. She also predicts that male control over women's reproduction and sexuality, part of the basis of women's oppression, will increase with the increasing popularity of the new reproductive technologies.

Elshtain, Jean Bethke. *Public Man, Private Woman: Women in Social and Political Thought*. Princeton, N.J.: Princeton University Press, 1981.

Scholarly survey and feminist analysis of women's place in political theory from Plato to contemporary feminist thought. Elshtain examines the Western tradition in terms of approaches to the public/private split and women's exclusion from public sphere. She argues for the central importance of family life and a feminist commitment to public discourse characterized by private values, insisting on the necessity of reconstructing public life as nonviolent and infused with the "politics of compassion." Bibliography.

Goldstein, Leslie Friedman. *The Constitutional Rights of Women: Cases in Law and Social Change*. Rev. ed. Madison: University of Wisconsin Press, 1988.
Detailed examination of legal cases concerning women's constitutional rights. Goldstein looks at all of the U.S. Supreme Court's decisions regarding gender, including cases about equal protection (of both women and men), gender discrimination, the vote, rape, the military, procreation and privacy issues (including abortion and federal funding for abortion), employment, and sexual harassment. Includes the full text of many major decisions, with discussion and analysis by Goldstein of legal and other implications for women and men. Considers not only gender issues but also issues connected to the meaning of the Supreme Court's power. "Case Questions" are included for many of the cases discussed. An appendix discusses how the Supreme Court operates; another reprints the U.S. Constitution.

Harrison, Cynthia. *On Account of Sex: The Politics of Women's Issues, 1945-1968*. Berkeley: University of California Press, 1988.
A history of political issues involving women, beginning with the aftermath of World War II and including examinations of the influence of the liberalism of the early 1960's and the impact of the Kennedy Administration and the President's Commission on the Status of Women (1961-1963). Harrison examines the strategies of presidents, political parties, and women activists in dealing with women's status and related political issues, and the impact of federal legislation and executive orders on the development of the contemporary women's movement. She sees the Presidential Commission as the centerpiece of Kennedy's approach to women's issues, and argues that the actions of the federal government made the women's movement more broad-based. Appendices reprint the Equal Pay Act of 1963, the Executive Order establishing the Presidential Commission, and members of committees of the Commission. Bibliography.

Hoff-Wilson, Joan, and Marjorie Lightman, eds. *Without Precedent: The Life and Career of Eleanor Roosevelt*. Bloomington: Indiana University Press, 1984.
Essays by historians to commemorate the centenary of Eleanor Roosevelt's birth. Contributors discuss her involvement in public affairs, from Democratic party politics and post-suffrage women's organizations to the United Nations

and the Civil Rights movement. Several essays debate Roosevelt's relationship to women's issues—including Lois Scharf's "ER and Feminism," which argues that her opposition to the ERA and her emphasis on individual rights and accomplishments characterize Roosevelt as a liberal reformer rather than a feminist. Contains a biographical sketch, with illustrations. All essays include short source lists. Index.

Klatch, Rebecca. *Women of the New Right*. Philadelphia: Temple University Press, 1987.

Study of women involved in a range of right-wing causes, not limited to women's issues. Klatch argues that these women fall into two distinct groups: "social" conservatives such as Phyllis Schlafly, who promote Christian values and the preservation of the traditional family, and "laissez-faire" conservatives, who emphasize individual rights and are often sympathetic to feminism. Includes anecdotes and excerpts from interviews with conservative women and detailed descriptions of the author's observation of political meetings and conventions.

Lenz, Elinor, and Barbara Myerhoff. *The Feminization of America: How Women's Values Are Changing Our Public and Private Lives*. Los Angeles: Jeremy P. Tarcher, 1985.

The authors examine women's current and potential impact on politics, society, and culture through their entry into the public world and the influence of "women's values" (including nurturance, capacity for intimacy, empathy, and integration), fostered through women's social history of responsibility for protecting life. Antinuclear activism and the peace movement are described as the greatest challenges and the most important areas for change. Chapters discuss female friendship, the changing workplace, the family, and health care system.

Luker, Kristin. *Abortion and the Politics of Motherhood*. Berkeley: University of California Press, 1984.

Major study of the pro-choice and antiabortion movements in the United States. Although intended to illuminate specific issues concerning abortion, Luker's detailed examination of the motivations, attitudes, goals, and organizational techniques of committed activists provides insights into women's role in political movements. Includes considerations of political strategies and futures of the movements. Appendix on methodology and tables.

Mandel, Ruth B. *In the Running: The New Woman Candidate*. New York: Ticknor & Fields, 1981. Reprint. Boston: Beacon Press, 1983.

Mandel uses firsthand accounts to examine the experiences and impact of women political candidates. Focuses on changes since the major breakthrough of the 1970's, when more women ran for office than ever before. Discusses image, the double standard, the role of private life, sexism, fundraising, the impact of the feminist movement, and women's organizations. Mandel argues that most women candidates are not explicitly feminists and often avoid emphasizing their identity as women but that more women in public office will have a major effect. She stresses the importance of women's participation in the political process.

Martin, George. *Madame Secretary: Frances Perkins*. Boston: Houghton Mifflin, 1976.

Biography of Perkins (1880-1965), the first woman cabinet member—Franklin Delano Roosevelt's Secretary of Labor from 1933 to 1945. Martin's study, which draws extensively on unpublished materials and family papers, begins with Perkins' appointment and organized labor's negative reaction to it, then traces her life from childhood on. Chapters address her education, experience in the New York State Labor Department, her marriage and family life, involvement in social and political issues—including settlement work and maternal health projects—and her activities after Roosevelt's death. Includes discussions of her efforts as secretary on behalf of Social Security and the minimum wage. Bibliography includes published and unpublished sources, interviews, and oral histories. Illustrations.

Newland, Kathleen. "Women in Politics." In her *The Sisterhood of Man*. New York: W. W. Norton, 1979.

An assessment of women's participation in politics around the world. Newland begins with a brief history of changes since World War II, then surveys women as voters, politicians, bureaucrats, and officeholders, and women's unofficial influence on political matters. Includes cross-cultural discussion of conflicts between the traditional view of politics as an inappropriate arena for women and recent changes in women's political roles. Tables.

Romney, Ronna, and Beppie Harrison. *Momentum: Women in American Politics Now*. New York: Crown, 1988.

Discussion of women's participation in politics in the 1970's and 1980's, drawing on the experiences of lobbyists, organizers, fundraisers, and women candidates and officeholders from both the Republican and Democratic parties. Includes chapters on how and why women enter politics, obstacles to their success, financial considerations, and attitudes of men and women toward female candidates and officeholders. The authors speculate that gender will continue to be a factor in future elections, but that its importance will decrease as women candidates become more commonplace.

Sapiro, Virginia. *The Political Integration of Women: Roles, Socialization, and Politics*. Urbana: University of Illinois Press, 1983.

Social science exploration of connections between women's private and political roles and the processes by which women are moving from a marginalized position to integration into active political life. Sapiro emphasizes the public nature of so-called private issues (such as child care) and uses empirical data to argue that their roles as mothers and wives have little if any effect on the political attitudes and behaviors of women as a group. Tables. Bibliographic essay.

Women and Education

Aisenberg, Nadyna, and Mona Harrington. *Women of Academe: Outsiders in the Sacred Grove*. Amherst: University of Massachusetts Press, 1988.
Study of women's experience with academic institutions, based on interviews with sixty women academics. The authors, both independent scholars, consider why so few women succeed ("success" being loosely defined as getting tenure at a major academic institution), concluding that women's experience is characterized by professional marginalization and exclusion from the centers of academic power. The study argues that women not only are discriminated against but also see their academic careers in terms of love for the work, rather than planning and considering goals and professional requirements. They recommend that women learn about the status of women in the profession (rather than accepting the myth of the academy as an ivory tower), seek support and information about gender issues from other women, and plan strategically for their careers. "Epilogue: Four Lives" provides personal accounts by four women academics. Appendix gives background data on interviewees.

Bowles, Gloria, and Renate Duelli Klein. "Introduction: Theories of Women's Studies and the Autonomy/Integration Debate." In *Theories of Women's Studies*, edited by Gloria Bowles and Renate Duelli Klein. Boston: Routledge & Kegan Paul, 1983.
A discussion of the debate over whether women's studies should be integrated into the traditional disciplines across the curriculum or established as an independent field. Bowles and Duelli Klein argue that autonomous programs have the potential to transform traditional knowledge and study through their focus on women's experience and understanding. Also includes brief review of theories of women's studies.

Burstyn, Joan N. *Victorian Education and the Ideal of Womanhood*. New York: Barnes & Noble Books, 1980. Reprint. New Brunswick, N.J.: Rutgers University Press, 1984.
Study of the Victorian ideology of separate spheres (the public world of work and politics for men, opposed to the private world of home and family for

women), focusing on disputes over higher education for women. Burstyn argues that demands for higher education represented an attempt by middle- and upper-class women to break out of the domestic sphere, while opponents perceived education as an effective form of social control. Illustrations. Bibliography.

Culley, Margo, and Catherine Portuges, eds. *Gendered Subjects: The Dynamics of Feminist Teaching*. Boston: Routledge & Kegan Paul, 1985.
Essays on feminist pedagogy by women and men, emphasizing the complexities of feminism's relationship to traditional teaching methods and educational institutions. Contributors address politics in the classroom, feminist challenges to traditional academic disciplines, racial and sexual identity, and teaching about theory. Essays include Adrienne Rich's "Taking Women Students Seriously," Janice G. Raymond's "Women's Studies: A Knowledge of One's Own," and Susan Stanford Friedman's "Authority in the Feminist Classroom: A Contradiction in Terms?" Selected bibliography and index.

Dzeich, Billie Wright, and Linda Weiner. *The Lecherous Professor: Sexual Harassment on Campus*. Boston: Beacon Press, 1984.
Study of sexual harassment of women students by male college and university faculty. Chapters address differences and similarities between harassment on campus and elsewhere; behavior of male professors; attitudes and responses of women faculty; and methods for preventing and dealing with harassment. The authors argue that women faculty have failed to organize effectively against harassment of their female students; they draw heavily on personal accounts, including excerpts from other studies. The final chapter provides recommendations for prevention and response, including grievance procedures, organized into separate lists of guidelines for students, parents, faculty, and college and university administrators. Appendices reprint the federal government's Title VII guidelines; a student's guide to legal remedies (including drawbacks of individual laws); a statement on sexual harassment from the president of Rutgers University; a sample sexual harassment policy from the University of Minnesota; and an outline for developing college and university guidelines and policies.

Faragher, John Mack, and Florence Howe, eds. *Women and Higher Education in American History: Essays from the Mount Holyoke College Sesquicentennial Symposia*. New York: W. W. Norton, 1988.
Collection of essays exploring aspects of women's higher education. Topics include historical attitudes toward education for women, contributions of prominent women educators, higher education for black women, the history of coeducation, and the impact of the women's movement. Ruth Schmidt's "The Role of Women's Colleges in the Future" argues that social and educational

inequities mean women's colleges still provide an important institutional haven. Index.

Fox, Lynn H., Linda Brody, and Dianne Tobin, eds. *Women and the Mathematical Mystique*. Baltimore: Johns Hopkins University Press, 1980.
Essays on women and mathematics. Includes information on professional women mathematicians, discussion of math as an academic discipline, and analyses of math education in schools and at the college level. Authors analyze differences in math achievement between boys and girls and men and women, focusing mostly on talented students for whom math is a plausible higher education goal or professional specialty. The collection includes studies of gifted girls and suggestions for increasing women's math achievements. Fox's conclusion summarizes the research and suggestions directed toward the future.

Hoffman, Nancy, ed. *Woman's "True" Profession: Voices from the History of Teaching*. Old Westbury, N.Y.: Feminist Press, 1981.
An anthology of writings by women—letters, diary excerpts, autobiography, and essays—dealing with their experiences of teaching through the early twentieth century. Examines rural and urban schools, black and white teachers, and includes writing by educational pioneers such as Emma Willard and Catherine Beecher. Illustrations. Contains a bibliography and an index.

Horowitz, Helen Lefkowitz. *Alma Mater: Design and Experience in the Women's Colleges from Their Nineteenth-Century Beginnings to the 1930s*. Boston: Beacon Press, 1984.
Horowitz examines the development of women's colleges, focusing on college life—traditions, social events, friendships, and so on—and its influence on the planning and construction of particular schools. Although much of the book deals with architectural and other design decisions, sections on dormitory life, dances, and other social components of college life provide insights into attitudes toward women's education and other aspects of life in the period. Illustrations.

——— . "College Women and Coeds." In her *Campus Life: Undergraduate Cultures from the End of the Eighteenth Century to the Present*. Chicago: University of Chicago Press, 1987.
An exploration of the experience of female undergraduates from the 1830's, when women first entered institutions of higher education. Horowitz describes early women undergraduates as pioneers with a serious commitment to their education and careers, and throughout the nineteenth century, a large percentage remained single, while in the twentieth century, the number who married rose gradually. The chapter considers differences and similarities between

women-only and coeducational schools, the impact of students' economic origins, male students' efforts to create a male-centered college life that excluded women, changes in social and other codes (including shifting sexual attitudes), the development of sororities, and women students' political attitudes. Illustrations.

Howe, Florence. *Myths of Coeducation: Selected Essays, 1964-1983*. Bloomington: Indiana University Press, 1984.
Essays by Howe, a longtime teacher and the founder of the Feminist Press, discuss a wide range of education-related issues, from her experience as a teacher in the civil rights movement's "freedom schools" to the development of women's studies and feminist scholarship. The title essay explores the nineteenth century "myths" surrounding university coeducation (for example, that the presence of women on college campuses would lead to immorality), and argues that, though women's studies is a corrective to the traditional "men's curriculum," the future will bring a genuinely "coeducational" course of study. Each essay is introduced by a headnote explaining its origins and publishing history.

Komarovsky, Mirra. *Women in College: Shaping New Feminine Identities*. New York: Basic Books, 1985.
Study of college women based on a four-year research project involving questionnaires, quantitative data collection, personal interviews, and diaries. Komarovsky's goal is to examine the impact of the college experience on young women's "life-style preferences," particularly the relative importance they place on career, marriage, and motherhood. Individual sections discuss young women's transition to college life (including joining the college community, changing self-concepts); the "Great Decisions" about career, marriage, and motherhood (focusing on changes in the student's attitudes from freshman to senior year); and the changing roles of women and men (including sexual and other relationships with men and attitudes toward the women's movement). The book makes extensive use of quotations from the project interviews and includes recommendations on college policies. Appendix describes the methodology of the study and reprints the questionnaire. Bibliography.

Langland, Elizabeth, and Walter Gove, eds. *A Feminist Perspective in the Academy: The Difference It Makes*. Chicago: University of Chicago Press, 1983.
Essays by prominent scholars in a variety of disciplines—including literature, religion, history, political science, economics, and psychology—discuss the impact of feminist scholarship on traditional academic study. In general, contributors argue that change has come very slowly and that, while some individ-

ual disciplines have made room for the study of women, the feminist perspective has yet to transform their fundamental premises or curriculum.

LaNoue, George R., and Barbara A. Lee. *Academics in Court: The Consequences of Faculty Discrimination Litigation*. Ann Arbor: University of Michigan Press, 1987.
Examination of faculty discrimination suits against colleges and universities, including those brought for sex discrimination. In addition to an overview of various grounds for suits, the litigation climate, and relevant legislation, chapters include case studies of individual women (and minority men). Tables and appendix listing discrimination cases from 1969 to 1984. Bibliography.

Lasser, Carol, ed. *Educating Men and Women Together: Coeducation in a Changing World*. Urbana: University of Illinois Press, 1987.
Essays presented at a conference celebrating the 150th anniversary of Oberlin College, the first coeducational college in the United States. Contributors examine coeducation, including questions about the continued usefulness of women's colleges; the history of women's education; and gender, race, and class issues. John D'Emilio considers sexual preference among college students; Mirra Komarovsky discusses gender roles among college men. Includes essays on "the Oberlin experience."

Newland, Kathleen. "Progress by Degrees: Education and Equality." In her *The Sisterhood of Man*. New York: W. W. Norton, 1979.
Discussion of girls' and women's access to education around the world. Newland examines literacy rates and their meaning, higher education for women, women as teachers, and the overall impact of education on women's status. She argues that for many women, improvement in their educational opportunities not only increases specific skills but also provides the women with a foothold in the world beyond family and local community. Tables.

Rich, Adrienne. "Toward a Woman-Centered University" and "Claiming an Education." In her *On Lies, Secrets, and Silence: Selected Prose, 1966-1978*. New York: W. W. Norton, 1979.
Influential essays calling for the transformation of attitudes toward women and education and of women's ideas about themselves as learners. "Toward a Woman-Centered University" urges that universities be sensitive to women's needs, including the provision of child care, the elimination of sexual hierarchies, discrimination and harassment, the recognition of women's contributions, and reform of the curriculum. "Claiming an Education" argues that women need to take themselves seriously as students by participating actively in their own education, rejecting stereotypes of women as passive, and demanding a woman-centered curriculum.

Rossiter, Margaret W. *Women Scientists in America: Struggles and Strategies to 1940*. Baltimore: Johns Hopkins University Press, 1982.
A history of women's experience as scientists and the limits placed on their access to adequate science education and academic employment. Rossiter discusses the importance of women's colleges as a rare source of serious science education, segregation in coeducational universities, the impact of increasing specialization, and the demand for greater professionalization. Illustrations, figures, tables. Bibliography includes lists of manuscript collections and oral histories.

Rothman, Sheila M. "The Ideology of Educated Motherhood." In her *Woman's Proper Sphere: A History of Changing Ideals and Practices, 1870 to the Present*. New York: Basic Books, 1978.
Rothman traces the Progressive Era's doctrine of "educated motherhood," which argued that children's complicated developmental needs required mothers trained in childrearing and which dictated major changes in social policy. Includes a discussion of the settlement house movement, the development of kindergartens, and the rise of women's higher education.

Scott, Anne Firor. "The Ever-Widening Circle: The Diffusion of Feminist Values from the Troy Female Seminary," "Education of Women: The Ambiguous Reform," and "Education and the Contemporary Woman." In her *Making the Invisible Woman Visible*. Urbana: University of Illinois Press, 1984.
Essays on the history of women's education in America, from the early nineteenth century Troy Female Seminary (the first permanent American school offering women the standard "male" curriculum) to twentieth century views. In "Education of Women," Scott argues that, though women have achieved educational equality, their training has been seen as separate from their potential achievement in larger society, as opposed to the definition of men's education as the route to advances in employment.

Simeone, Angela. *Academic Women: Working Towards Equality*. Foreword by Jesse Bernard. South Hadley, Mass.: Bergin & Garvey, 1987.
Simeone examines the effects of recent attempts to achieve equality for women faculty in higher education, emphasizing progress that has been made since the 1964 publication of Jesse Bernard's *Academic Women*. Using a wide range of studies to explore larger trends, and interviews with individual women faculty, chapters address career choice; measures of formal status (such as statistics on salary, rank, and tenure, and affirmative action programs); teacher and researcher roles; informal relationships among women academics (from their place in the "old boys' networks" to the development of feminist networks); sponsors and protégés; and marital status and family life. Conclusion asserts

that improvement—such as policies on discrimination, and greater institutional support for women—have come about partly because of organizing by women faculty themselves, and emphasizes the positive impact of relationships among faculty women. Bibliography.

Solomon, Barbara Miller. *In the Company of Educated Women: A History of Women and Higher Education in America*. New Haven, Conn.: Yale University Press, 1985.
Solomon surveys women's access to higher education from Colonial times to the present. She focuses on the ways that women's demands for education reshaped the curriculum and educational institutions themselves and makes connections between the feminist movement and the growth of higher education for women. The study highlights important breakthroughs, such as the first women's entrance into medical and divinity schools and the development of colleges for black women. Illustrations. Tables providing enrollment and employment statistics. Bibliography.

Weiler, Kathleen. *Women Teaching for Change: Gender, Class, and Power*. Introduction by Henry A. Giroux and Paulo Freire. South Hadley, Mass.: Bergin & Garvey, 1988.
A scholarly study of feminist public high-school teachers. Weiler critiques both traditional educational theorists and previous feminist analyses, defining school as the intersection of social, institutional, and personal forces. Much of the discussion is highly theoretical but draws extensively on detailed examples from the classroom, including transcriptions of exchanges among students and between students and teachers over issues of gender, race, and class. Weiler argues that feminist pedagogy has the potential to transform educational institutions and offers lessons for other critical pedagogies.

Wells, Anna Mary. *Miss Marks and Miss Woolley*. Boston: Houghton Mifflin, 1978.
A joint biography of Mary Emma Woolley, president of Mt. Holyoke College from 1901 to 1937, and her longtime companion Jeannette Marks, chair of the college's English literature department. Wells focuses on their roles as pioneers in promoting American higher education for women—both as activists in the cause and as early examples of women academics—including their dedication to women's education as a feminist concern alongside other issues such as the Equal Rights Amendment. She presents their relationship as intimate, if not necessarily overtly sexual, and emphasizes the conflicts between Woolley's popularity and Marks's reputation as a difficult person, a situation that made their contemporaries view Marks as "a necessary evil" in Woolley's life. Illustrations.

Biographies and Autobiographies

Abramson, Jill, and Barbara Franklon. *Where They Are Now: The Story of the Women of Harvard Law, 1974*. Garden City, N.Y.: Doubleday, 1986.
A study of the women graduates of Harvard Law School's class of 1974. Begins with an outline of changes at Harvard, such as the "new breed" of students influenced by the political movements of the 1960's, and changing attitudes toward women students at the law school. Subsequent chapters examine the progress—or lack of it—of the women's careers in the decade since graduation, including the issues involved in negotiating between professional and personal lives, progress through corporations and law firms, and those who have withdrawn entirely from the practice of law. Includes a statistical profile of the 1974 women graduates of Harvard Law. Bibliography.

Akers, Charles W. *Abigail Adams: An American Woman*. Boston: Little, Brown, 1980.
Biography of a woman famous not only as the wife of one president and the mother of another but also as an early promoter of women's rights and, in Akers' view, a person whose life is "a large window on society" during the early history of the United States. Includes discussion of her famous "Remember the Ladies" letter to husband John Adams, urging him not to support the Constitutional granting of unlimited authority to men.

Alexander, Maxine, ed. *Speaking for Ourselves: Women of the South*. New York: Pantheon Books, 1984.
A collection of personal and historical essays, oral histories and interviews, poetry and fiction by women about life in the South over the past fifty years. Includes a wide range of voices by class, race, and age, and addresses many issues, including growing up, family, mother-daughter relationships and other bonds among women, work, sexuality, and home. Contributors include academics, artists and writers, and political activists. Illustrations.

Angelou, Maya. *I Know Why the Caged Bird Sings*. New York: Random House, 1969. Reprint. New York: Bantam Books, 1970.
First volume of autobiography by black writer and performer. Angelou focuses on her childhood and adolescence, including her experiences of poverty, racism, and sexual abuse. Later volumes—*Gather Together in My Name* (Random House, 1974), *Singin' and Swingin' and Gettin' Merry Like Christmas* (Random House, 1976), and *All God's Children Need Traveling Shoes* (Random House, 1986)—describe her development as a poet and essayist, actress, and dancer, her growing identification with the Civil Rights movement, and her experience living in Ghana.

Baker, Jean H. *Mary Todd Lincoln: A Biography*. New York: W. W. Norton, 1987.
Biography of a woman Baker sees as both exceptional (because of her high
status, formal education, and marriage to a president) and accepting of conventional ideas about women, even those that conflicted with her own personality
and behavior. Baker explores Lincoln's life as it illuminates the family dynamics of the period, particularly the tensions between convention and confor-
mity, but also tries to counter popular stereotypes of her as a shrew. Early
chapters trace her family background.

Bataille, Gretchen M., and Kathleen Muller Sands. *American Indian Women: Tell-
ing Their Lives*. Lincoln: University of Nebraska Press, 1984.
A study of autobiographies and personal narratives by Native American
women. The authors deal with both the written and oral traditions (including
accounts collected through ethnographic studies) and a variety of Indian nations. Chapters trace the literary tradition and look at specific women's narratives. A lengthy annotated bibliography includes both published and manuscript citations, grouped into autobiographies, biographies, ethnographic and
historical studies, and critical studies.

Bateson, Mary Catherine. *With a Daughter's Eye: A Memoir of Margaret Mead and
Gregory Bateson*. New York: William Morrow, 1984.
An account of growing up as the daughter of world-renowned anthropologists.
Bateson describes both her childhood and adult relationships with her parents,
including Mead's cultural impact as a writer on motherhood (based on observations in the field, which she also applied to her daughter's upbringing). She
also addresses the effects of her parents' separation and divorce; her relationship with her "Aunt Marie"—Mead's college friend—who served as a constant parental figure for the young Bateson; and her role in adulthood when, as
a trained anthropologist, she became her parents' colleague. Includes reflections on Mead and Bateson as both parents and anthropologists. Illustrations.

Boller, Paul F., Jr. *Presidential Wives*. New York: Oxford University Press, 1988.
Anecdotal history of America's First Ladies, from Martha Washington to
Nancy Reagan. Each chapter begins with biographical information, emphasizing the woman's relationship with her husband, and most entries recount
several anecdotes. Chapters include discussions of education, political activity
if any, and family life. Index.

Brough, James. *Princess Alice: A Biography of Alice Roosevelt Longworth*. Boston:
Little, Brown, 1975.
Biography of President Theodore Roosevelt's daughter (1884-1980), famous for
flouting the era's conventions for ladylike behavior. Includes discussion of her
life in the White House, her marriage to Ohio representative Nicholas Long-

worth (who later became Speaker of the House), and her political involvements. Illustrations.

Cantarow, Ellen, et al. *Moving the Mountain*. New York: McGraw-Hill, 1980.
Oral histories of three women activists: Florence Luscomb (born 1887), who worked for suffrage, labor, and peace; Ella Baker (born 1903), who worked for civil rights; and Jessie Lopez de la Cruz (born 1919), who worked for farmworkers' rights. Introductions to each woman's story, chronologies, and time line provide personal and historical contexts. Illustrations. Bibliography.

Chestnut, Mary Boykin. *A Diary from Dixie*. Edited by Ben Amer Williams. Boston: Houghton Mifflin, 1949. Reprint. Cambridge, Mass.: Harvard University Press, 1980.
Extensive excerpts from an important diary kept by an aristocratic Southern woman (died 1886) during the Civil War. Entries cover 1861 to 1865 and describe social and family life, politics, and the effects of the war. Introduction provides the history of Chestnut's diary, identifies major figures mentioned in entries; occasional footnotes explain colloquialisms and obscure references. Chestnut has long been seen as a feminist and abolitionist, but that interpretation of her attitudes has recently come under attack. Index.

Coles, Robert, and Jane Hallowell Coles. *Women of Crisis*. Vol. 1, *Lives of Struggle and Hope*. New York: Delacorte Press, 1978. Vol. 2, *Lives of Work and Dreams*. New York: Delacorte Press, 1980.
Popular oral history consisting of biographical portraits and personal narratives of "ordinary" women. The Coles' subjects reflect on daily life, work, family, and their involvement in political movements (civil rights and feminism). The selection of subjects reflects a variety of ethnic and racial identities, classes, and regions.

Craft, Christine. *Too Old, Too Ugly, and Not Deferential to Men: An Anchorwoman's Courageous Battle Against Sex Discrimination*. Santa Barbara, Calif.: Capra Press, 1986. Reprint with new introduction. Rocklin, Calif.: Prima Publishing, 1988.
Television anchorwoman Craft's account of her nationally publicized sex discrimination suit against the Kansas City television station that fired her on grounds she and many others believe were unfair. (Although the initially successful suit was eventually overturned, Craft continues to work in television news.) The book focuses on the details of the lawsuit, but Craft also comments on television news in general, especially her perception that station owners and producers are more concerned with appearance than expertise. Illustrations.

Duster, Alfreda M., ed. *Crusade for Justice: The Autobiography of Ida B. Wells*. Chicago: University of Chicago Press, 1970.

Autobiography of the black activist (1862-1931) who fought against racial injustice, edited by her daughter. Born in slavery, Wells became a teacher and writer, worked against discrimination in employment and transportation and on antilynching campaigns, and helped to organize the National Association for the Advancement of Colored People (NAACP). Her memoirs describe her private life as well as her public career.

Felsenthal, Carol. *Phyllis Schlafly: The Sweetheart of the Silent Majority*. Chicago: Regnery Gateway, 1981.
Biography of America's most prominent antifeminist activist, best known for her campaign against the Equal Rights Amendment. Felsenthal's account includes chapters on both Schlafly's family life and her political activities. The conclusion identifies Schlafly as "a power to be reckoned with" in the future. Illustrations.

Franklin, Penelope, ed. *Private Pages: Diaries of American Women, 1830-1970s*. New York: Ballantine, 1986.
Excerpts from diaries of "ordinary" American women, arranged in life-cycle order so that, taken together, they trace women's experience from adolescence to old age. Most concentrate on adolescence through middle age and reflect on family, friends, romance, and larger political and social issues. Included is the diary of a Japanese-American woman, written in an internment camp during World War II. Each woman's work includes a short introduction, explanatory notes, and an afterword, providing biographical information and situating the diary within her life. Editor's introduction discusses problems inherent in publishing diaries, including issues of privacy and editing, and considers why women keep diaries. Excerpts preserve their authors' original grammar and style. Illustrations.

Hellman, Lillian. *An Unfinished Woman: A Memoir*. Boston: Little, Brown, 1969.
The first volume of autobiography by playwright Hellman, author of *The Little Foxes* and other plays. The memoir's focus is on her childhood, education, development as a writer, radical political involvements, and her thirty-year relationship with writer Dashiell Hammett, and ends with his death. Includes descriptions of Hellman's experiences during the Spanish Civil War and World War II, including her visits to the Soviet Union during and after the war.

Honig, Emily, and Gail Hershatter. *Personal Voices: Chinese Women in the 1980s*. Stanford, Calif.: Stanford University Press, 1988.
Study of women in contemporary China, emphasizing their personal experiences and recent public controversies over changes in women's lives. Chapters are arranged according to the life cycle: growing up, sexuality, friendship and

courtship, marriage, family relationships, divorce, work, violence against women, and "feminist voices." Each chapter ends with translations from Chinese publications on the topic under discussion, drawing on everything from personal accounts to official policies and quoting publications that range from popular magazines and advice books to government pamphlets. Illustrations. Bibliography includes sources in both English and Chinese.

Lamb, Patricia Frazer, and Kathryn Joyce Hohlwein. *Touchstones: Letters Between Two Women, 1953-1964*. Edited by Lamb. New York: Harper & Row, 1983.
Representative letters from twelve years of correspondence between college friends living far apart. The letters focus particularly on marriage, including problems with husbands, but also examine family, friendship, and sexuality. The collection provides a useful and highly personalized reflection of changing times and attitudes toward women and a vivid portrait of women's friendship. Introduction and afterword by Lamb provide biographical background.

L'Engle, Madeleine. *Two-Part Invention: The Story of a Marriage*. New York: Farrar, Straus & Giroux, 1988.
Memoirs by the author of the children's classic *A Wrinkle in Time*. The focus is on L'Engle's marriage to actor Hugh Franklin, their family life in New England, her religious faith, and his gradual death from cancer. The book includes much discussion of their careers, including her thoughts on writing.

Morris, Jan. *Conundrum*. New York: Harcourt Brace Jovanovich, 1974.
The autobiography of a male journalist who had a much-publicized sex-change operation. In addition to illuminating attitudes toward gender identity and sexuality, Morris' experience of both male and female life provides insights into sex roles, such as the acknowledgment that "the more I was treated as a woman, the more woman I became."

Murray, Pauli. *Song in a Weary Throat: An American Pilgrimage*. New York: Harper & Row, 1987.
The autobiography of a remarkable and multifaceted black women: a civil rights activist, feminist, lawyer, teacher, poet, and one of the first women ordained as an Episcopal priest. Murray (1910-1985) describes her confrontations with racism and sexism—including racial and sexual discrimination in university admissions policies—her long friendship with Eleanor Roosevelt, civil rights work, participation in the founding of the National Organization for Women, political campaigns, and teaching career. Index. Illustrations.

Nash, Alanna. *Golden Girl: The Story of Jessica Savitch*. New York: E. P. Dutton, 1988.
The biography of one of the first women anchors on network television, who

died accidentally at the age of thirty-six. Nash insists that Savitch's beauty played a central role in her rise to prominence, and uses her to exemplify television news' focus on appearance over experience. She emphasizes not only Savitch's lack of journalistic skill but also the difficulties created by being thrust into a job for which she was not prepared, and examines her unhappy personal life—particularly her relationships with men—and drug abuse. Illustrations.

Pryor, Elizabeth Brown. *Clara Barton: Professional Angel*. Philadelphia: University of Pennsylvania Press, 1987.
A biography of Barton (1821-1912), the founder of the American Red Cross. Drawing for the first time on her personal diaries, letters, and other unpublished materials, Pryor emphasizes the woman behind the myth of selfless devotion to helping others. She focuses on Barton's emotional isolation from friends and family, her struggle to become an important person in contradiction to standards of appropriate feminine behavior, and her several nervous breakdowns. Pryor argues that work gave Barton's life a purpose, and although mythologized as an altruist, she actually needed the praise and appreciation that came from her celebrated role as an "angel." Illustrations.

Roosevelt, Eleanor. *The Autobiography of Eleanor Roosevelt*. New York: Harper & Row, 1961. Reprint with new introduction. Boston: G. K. Hall, 1984.
One-volume condensation of Roosevelt's three-volume autobiography. The book covers her childhood, her marriage to Franklin D. Roosevelt, his terms as Governor of New York and President of the United States, and Eleanor Roosevelt's political work after his death (including her role in the United Nations).

Sarton, May. *After the Stroke: A Journal*. New York: W. W. Norton, 1988.
One of a series of published journals and memoirs by the poet and novelist (born 1912), author of *Mrs. Stevens Hears the Mermaids Singing*. This one covers the period from April, 1986, to February, 1987, and describes the aftereffects of a stroke Sarton suffered in February, 1986. She describes both the stroke and her recovery and includes reflections on growing old, illness, and her personal life, as well as thoughts on outside events. Illustrations.

Saywell, Shelley. *Women in War*. New York: Viking Penguin, 1985.
Firsthand accounts of women's experience in war and wartime from World War II to El Salvador and the Falkland Islands. Includes accounts by and about women in and out of the armed forces and on both sides of the conflicts, working as pilots, nurses, reporters, formal soldiers, and guerrillas, behind and at the front lines. Chapters are organized by wars, including World War II (with separate chapters by theater of battle), the 1948 war of Israeli independence, and Vietnam. Illustrations. Bibliography.

Schilpp, Madelon, and Sharon M. Murphy. *Great Women of the Press*. Carbondale: Southern Illinois University Press, 1983.

Short biographies of American women journalists from the eighteenth to the twentieth century, beginning with Elizabeth Timothy (1700-1757), the first woman publisher in the United States. Chapters describe both personal and professional lives, participation in politics (including women's issues), and contributions to the development of American journalism. Among subjects are civil rights activist Ida B. Wells-Barnett (1862-1931) and photojournalist Margaret Bourke-White (1904-1971). Bibliography includes works by and about subjects. Index.

Scott, Anne Firor. "The Biographical Mode." In her *Making the Invisible Woman Visible*. Urbana: University of Illinois Press, 1984.

Essays on writing women's biographies, along with biographical essays depicting specific women from the eighteenth to the twentieth century by a prominent historian of women. The section includes "Self-Portraits: Three Women," about three "ordinary" eighteenth century women, and an essay on settlement house activist Jane Addams.

Sklar, Kathryn Kish. *Catharine Beecher: A Study in American Domesticity*. New Haven, Conn.: Yale University Press, 1973.

The biography of the influential teacher, religious writer, and supporter of women's education (1800-1878)—best known today as the sister of Harriet Beecher Stowe. Catharine Beecher's *Treatise on Domestic Economy* was one of the period's most important examples of the ideology of domesticity. Sklar argues that Beecher, who opposed the movement for women's rights, expressed her rebellion against male domination indirectly by developing an ideology that gave women a central place in national life through the definition of home and family as the central social unit. Illustrations.

Smith, Margaret Chase. *Declaration of Conscience*. Garden City, N.Y.: Doubleday, 1972.

Memoirs of the first woman elected to both the House of Representatives and the U.S. Senate. Framed by two "declarations"—the first (1950) against Senator Joseph McCarthy's witchhunts, the second (1970) against New Left violence. Includes a discussion of the evolution of her beliefs, her experience as a U.S. Senator, and chapters on women's issues (highlighting Smith's involvement in legislation on women in the armed forces). Appendices reprint assorted statements by Smith.

Steinem, Gloria. *Marilyn*. New York: Henry Holt, 1986.

A photobiography of actress Marilyn Monroe, focusing on the lasting effects of childhood sexual abuse and other forms of victimization. Steinem sees Monroe as a particularly extreme representative of women's experience and describes her life as a constant and unsuccessful struggle to negotiate the tensions between her image as a child-woman and sex symbol—the "Marilyn Monroe" the public knew—and the isolation and loss felt by the woman she identifies by Monroe's real name, Norma Jeane. Illustrations.

_____ . *Outrageous Acts and Everyday Rebellions*. New York: Holt, Rinehart & Winston, 1983.
A collection of essays by feminist Gloria Steinem (founding editor of *Ms.* magazine), many of them previously published. Among them are several personal accounts, including stories about the development of her commitment to feminism; considerations of individual women such as Marilyn Monroe and Alice Walker, and of political issues from work, women and language, and pornography to media representations of genitally mutilated women. "Ruth's Song (Because She Could Not Sing It)" is a moving account of Steinem's adolescence as the daughter of a mentally ill mother. Index.

Stenn, David. *Clara Bow: Runnin' Wild*. Garden City, N.Y.: Doubleday, 1988.
Biography of actress Clara Bow (1905-1965), the "It" girl who embodied 1920's notions of sex appeal. Emphasis is on her unhappy and often violent early life, her rapid rise to fame as one of America's first film stars, her flamboyant life-style, implication in sexual scandals in the 1920's, her money problems, and her life after stardom passed. Sources include interviews with Bow's contemporaries and archival materials. Illustrations.

Wexler, Alice. *Emma Goldman in America*. Boston: Beacon Press, 1984.
Biography of the influential anarchist and Socialist (1869-1940), from her childhood in Lithuania to her 1919 deportation from the United States for her activism. Includes a discussion of Goldman's insistence on attention to women's issues at a time when many of her comrades saw such topics as secondary to the goal of Socialist revolution.

Wilder, Laura Ingalls, and Rose Wilder Lane. *A Little House Sampler*. Edited by William T. Anderson. Lincoln: University of Nebraska Press, 1988.
A collection of autobiographical writings by Wilder, the author of the *Little House* series, and her daughter. The book is arranged chronologically and includes essays, newspaper articles, and fictional excerpts. Editor's introductions to many entries explain biographical and historical background, and a biographical epilogue provides information about Wilder's and Lane's later years. The women's writings provide vivid descriptions of life in the nineteenth and early twentieth century Midwest, including many of the events on which Wilder's novels are based. Illustrations.

THE WOMEN'S MOVEMENT

History of the Women's Movement

Becker, Susan D. *The Origins of the Equal Rights Amendment: American Feminism Between the Wars*. Westport, Conn.: Greenwood Press, 1981.
Study examining the post-suffrage women's movement and focusing on the promotion of the ERA by the National Women's Party (NWP), characterized here as the only "true" feminist organization of the period. Becker discusses NWP coalitions and conflicts with other women's groups, interwar hostility toward feminism, and flaws in the party's platform, including the failure to develop an effective theory of women's position. Selected bibliography lists manuscript collections and contemporary pamphlets.

DuBois, Ellen Carol. *Feminism and Suffrage: The Emergence of an Independent Women's Movement in America, 1848-1869*. Ithaca, N.Y.: Cornell University Press, 1978.
DuBois traces the origins of the American feminist movement, with an emphasis on early suffragists' close ties to the abolition movement. She argues that abolitionists' refusal, even after the Civil War, to take woman suffrage seriously forced Susan B. Anthony, Elizabeth Cady Stanton, and others to form an independent movement, but that feminism retained its character as a middle-class, largely white reform movement focused on the vote for the next fifty years. Bibliography includes useful list of manuscript collections.

DuBois, Ellen Carol, and Linda Gordon. "Seeking Ecstasy on the Battlefield: Danger and Pleasure in Nineteenth-Century Feminist Thought." In *Pleasure and Danger: Exploring Female Sexuality*, edited by Carol S. Vance. Boston: Routledge & Kegan Paul, 1984.
Authors argue that nineteenth century women reformers equated sexual freedom with danger and instead promoted "social purity" through the temperance movement and the campaign against prostitution. The essay outlines the problems this caused for ideas about female sexuality and the limits it imposed on the feminist movement. DuBois and Gordon also suggest links between these attitudes and some strains of the current women's movement.

Flexner, Eleanor. *Century of Struggle: The Woman's Rights Movement in the United States*. Cambridge, Mass.: Harvard University Press, 1959. Reprint, with new preface. New York: Atheneum, 1973.
Beginning with a survey of women's position before 1800, Flexner charts the history of the American women's movement up to the 1920 achievement of the vote. She argues that women had to resist their own and others' views of them

as primarily child bearers and child rearers, and she discusses women's participation in the abolition and labor movements, their role in higher education,
and conflicts among different suffrage organizations.

Lasser, Carol, and Marlene Deahl Merrill, eds. *Friends and Sisters: Letters Between
Lucy Stone and Antoinette Brown Blackwell, 1846-93*. Urbana: University of
Illinois Press, 1987.
Chronologically arranged letters document the close fifty-year friendship between these nineteenth century sisters-in-law, both prominent abolitionists and
feminists. (Stone became a major American suffrage leader, Blackwell the first
regularly ordained woman Protestant minister in the United States.) Includes a
general introduction. Also introductions to each section, explanatory footnotes
in each letter, and list of useful sources.

Lunardini, Christine A. *From Equal Suffrage to Equal Rights: Alice Paul and the
National Women's Party, 1910-1928*. New York: New York University Press,
1986.
History of the National Women's Party, a suffrage organization that continued
its work after women won the vote in 1920. Lunardini focuses on the leadership of Alice Paul and her efforts on behalf of the Equal Rights Amendment.
Appendix with text and legislative history of Nineteenth Amendment, which
granted women the vote, and texts of two versions of the ERA. Extensive
bibliography, including manuscript collections, oral history interviews with
suffragists, and relevant government publications.

Rossi, Alice S., ed. *The Feminist Papers: From Adams to de Beauvoir*. New York:
Columbia University Press, 1973. Reprint, with new introduction. Boston:
Northeastern University Press, 1988.
Excerpts from important speeches, essays, and other documents of the
women's movement from the eighteenth to the mid-twentieth century. Includes
writings on underlying philosophy, specific organizations, and the related abo-
lition and birth-control movements. Among the writers excerpted are Mary
Wollstonecraft, Margaret Fuller, John Stuart Mill, Emma Goldman, Margaret
Sanger, and Virginia Woolf. Rossi's introductions to each section provide historical and social contexts.

Scott, Anne Firor, and Andrew MacKay Scott. *One Half the People: The Fight for
Woman Suffrage*. Philadelphia: J. B. Lippincott, 1975. Reprint. Urbana: University of Illinois Press, 1982.
A brief history of the American suffrage movement. More than half the book
consists of documents and excerpts from magazine and newspaper articles,
letters, public testimony, and autobiographical writings.

Spender, Dale, ed. *Feminist Theorists: Three Centuries of Key Women Thinkers*. Introduction by Ellen Carol DuBois. New York: Pantheon Books, 1983.
A collection of essays on the ideas of important women—from Aphra Behn (1640-1689), the first professional woman writer, to French philosopher Simone de Beauvoir, author of the influential *The Second Sex*. Subjects are mainly British and American but include women from around the world, whose contributions range from literature to political theory and philosophy. Among the contributors are Ann J. Lane, Alix Kates Shulman, and Renate Duelli Klein. Bibliography.

Stanton, Elizabeth Cady. *Eighty Years and More: Reminiscences 1815-1897*. London: T. Fisher Unwin, 1898. Reprint. New York: Schocken Books, 1971.
The autobiography of one of the major American suffrage activists. Stanton recounts her childhood, marriage and family life, political activities, and world travels. She and recalls the struggle—unfinished at her death in 1902—for the enfranchisement of women. Index of names.

Strachey, Ray. *The Cause: A Short History of the Women's Movement in Great Britain*. London: G. Bell & Sons, 1928. Reprint. London: Virago, 1978.
Classic history of the British women's movement, from late eighteenth century efforts to improve women's legal status to the beginning of women's equal participation in government after World War I. Strachey, an active participant in the movement, covers women's entry into professional medicine, higher education, philanthropy, and local government. Discusses changes in social behavior, clothing, and even sports. Illustrations. Includes a reprint of Florence Nightingale's 1852 feminist essay "Cassandra" and a short bibliography.

Van Voris, Jacqueline. *Carrie Chapman Catt: A Public Life*. New York: Feminist Press at the City University of New York, 1987.
The biography of one of the most important activists for women's suffrage and peace (1859-1947). Catt was president of the National American Woman Suffrage Association and founder of the International Woman Suffrage Alliance and the League of Women Voters. Van Voris examines Catt's upbringing, her growth as a feminist leader, and her international work for women's rights and peace. Includes photographs and much new material on her travels to Europe, China, and South Africa. Bibliography and index.

Contemporary Women's Movement

Beauvoir, Simone de. *The Second Sex*. Translated by H. M. Parshley. New York: Alfred A. Knopf, 1953. Reprint. New York: Bantam Books, 1961.
One of the most important and influential twentieth century feminist analyses,

considered by many to be the first serious intellectual theory of women's
oppression. De Beauvoir bases her argument on existentialist philosophy,
claiming that the definition of women as the "Other" allows men to define
themselves as fully human, active agents. Although she assumes women's
biological difference from men, her analysis of history, literature, and politics
emphasizes the socially imposed limits on women's lives.

Berry, Mary Frances. *Why ERA Failed: Politics, Women's Rights, and the Amending
Process of the Constitution*. Bloomington: Indiana University Press, 1986.
Examination of the ERA defeat in the context of the history of the process of
amending the U.S. Constitution. Chapters define the process by describing the
history of the Sixteenth Amendment (authorizing Congress to impose income
tax) and the Nineteenth Amendment (granting women's suffrage), Prohibition's implementation and repeal, and the failure to implement a child-labor
amendment. Subsequent chapters discuss the pro- and anti-ERA campaigns,
comparing activists with those who fought for and against earlier amendments.
Berry, a former member of the U.S. Commission on Civil Rights, argues that
ERA proponents failed to learn lessons from past successful campaigns, especially the importance of developing a state-by-state consensus and persuading both voters and legislators of the necessity of equal rights as a principle;
and were victims of bad timing, trying to pass a controversial amendment in a
time of reaction rather than reform. Appendix reprints selected amendments
and proposals, including the ERA.

Davidson, Nicholas. *The Failure of Feminism*. Buffalo, N.Y.: Prometheus Books,
1988.
Davidson argues that feminists deny gender differences and are hostile toward
any manifestations of such differences (from fashion to separate career trajec-
tories). He insists that this has undermined any movement toward true equality. Although feminism is credited with important changes in women's status,
it is also described here as "a failure."

Donovan, Josephine. *Feminist Theory: The Intellectual Traditions of American Feminism*. New York: Frederick Ungar, 1985.
An examination of the impact of various philosophies on American feminism,
from eighteenth century Enlightenment to the 1980's. Donovan traces the influence of Marxism, Freudian theory, and existentialism; describes the development of "cultural" and radical feminism; and concludes with a look at the
recent rise of a "new feminist moral vision" exemplified by psychologist Carol
Gilligan. Selected bibliography covers a wide range of feminist theory.

Eisenstein, Hester. *Contemporary Feminist Thought*. Boston: G. K. Hall, 1983.
History and critique of American feminist theory, emphasizing connections

between radical feminism of the 1970's and the current work of Adrienne Rich, Nancy Chodorow, Mary Daly, and others. Eisenstein argues that some theorists have abandoned the original critique of socially constructed sex roles in favor of a vision of women's superiority. Includes discussions of the importance of lesbianism in feminist theory, the controversy over pornography and sado-masochism, and three chapters examining "the cultural meaning of mother-hood."

Evans, Sara. *Personal Politics: The Roots of the Women's Liberation Movement in the Civil Rights Movement and the New Left.* New York: Alfred A. Knopf, 1979. Reprint. New York: Vintage Books, 1980.
Traces the evolution of contemporary feminism from women's involvement in the civil rights movement of the 1960's. Evans argues that the frustration of women on the Left over their secondary position within the movement forced them to confront male activists about their sexism; eventually they formed a political movement of their own. Includes reprints of several important documents from the period.

Friedan, Betty. *The Feminine Mystique.* New York: W. W. Norton, 1963. Reprint. New York: Dell Books, 1970.
Often cited as the book that started the women's movement of the 1960's. Friedan describes the dilemma of the well-educated, middle-class American woman whose options are limited to marriage and motherhood. Although she does not question these roles, she insists that women should have careers as well. She provides an extremely influential analysis of the claustrophobia of suburban life and the effects on women of conventional media images and professional advice.

Hewlett, Sylvia Ann. "The Women's Movement." In her *A Lesser Life: The Myth of Women's Liberation in America.* New York: William Morrow, 1986.
Hewlett argues that American feminists' emphasis on equal rights actually undermines the struggle for pay equity, maternity leave, child care, and other provisions that would improve women's lives. The analysis is introduced by a personal essay recounting Hewlett's experiences of pregnancy, childbirth, and related work problems. This chapter is controversial in its attack on organized liberal and radical feminism.

Hoff-Wilson, Joan, ed. *Rights of Passage: The Past and Future of the ERA.* Bloomington: Indiana University Press, 1986.
Essays by historians grouped by subject: the origins and early disagreements over the Equal Rights Amendment, reasons for its defeat, and the significance of that defeat. Hoff-Wilson introduces the book and each group of essays,

describing the ERA as a symbol of the second women's movement equivalent to the function of the suffrage amendment in the first women's movement. Introduction to book outlines the history of equal rights movements and of women's constitutional rights. An appendix, "Various Attempts to Define Equal Rights for Women," reprints different versions of the ERA, proposed riders, and other relevant bills. Bibliography, index. Illustrations.

Klatch, Rebecca E. "Feminism." In her *Women of the New Right*. Philadelphia: Temple University Press, 1987.
Discusses attitudes toward feminism among women active in conservative causes. Klatch contrasts the "social conservative" view—in which feminism is seen as antifamily and an intrusion of big government—with "laissez-faire" support for pay equity and self-determination on issues such as abortion and homosexuality. She argues that conservative women justify their public activism by distinguishing mere "conventions" from more lasting and immutable "traditional values" and by presenting themselves as altruistic guardians of morality.

McAllister, Pam, ed. *Reweaving the Web of Life: Feminism and Nonviolence*. Philadelphia: New Society Publishers, 1982.
Essays, poems, personal statements, songs, and stories by women and men about feminism and nonviolence. Includes examinations of the relationship between the two movements. Contributors include singer-songwriters Holly Near and Joan Baez; writers Alice Walker, Sally Miller Gearhart, and Valerie Miner; and scholars, activists, and others. Writers address racism, women and the draft, pacifism, spirituality, historical figures, male sexuality and violence, ecology, and women's place in the natural world. Includes chronology of relevant events, particularly protests and peace actions, from 1600 to 1981. Illustrations. List of readings. Index.

Mansbridge, Jane J. *Why We Lost the ERA*. Chicago: University of Chicago Press, 1986.
Examination of the defeat of the ERA. Argues that both proponents and opponents exaggerated the ERA's potential effects and that pro-ERA forces were overly optimistic, used self-defeating tactics, and relied too much on "ideologically pure" volunteers. Mansbridge claims that the amendment would not actually have produced sweeping changes but emphasizes its importance as an embodiment of the principle of equality. Lack of serious national debate made the fight a "struggle over symbols," with Phyllis Schlafly's "STOP-ERA" movement successful at arousing controversy. Includes chapter on Illinois organizing efforts. Tables, figures. Appendix summarizing ERA support from 1970 to 1982.

Marks, Elaine, and Isabel de Courtivron, eds. *New French Feminisms: An Anthology*. Amherst: University of Massachusetts Press, 1980.
The first English-language collection of writings by recent French feminist theorists—and the book that introduced their controversial ideas to U.S. readers. Includes excerpts from important works by Hélène Cixous, Catherine Clément, Luce Irigaray, and Julia Kristeva. Editors' introductions trace the history of the French feminist and antifeminist movements and examine the controversies and intellectual contexts of specific ideas. The selections and excerpts themselves range from straightforward political manifestos to complex theoretical analyses filled with elaborate wordplay. "Bio/Bibliography" provides capsule information about contributors. Selected bibliography.

Millett, Kate. *Sexual Politics*. Garden City, N.Y.: Doubleday, 1969.
One of the first radical feminist theories and literary analyses of the modern movement. Using literature by Norman Mailer, Henry Miller, and others, Millett argues that Western culture denigrates women, reducing them to sexual objects. She insists on an understanding of the power relations between the sexes ("sexual politics") as a route to women's liberation from male constraints.

Mitchell, Juliet, and Ann Oakley, eds. *What Is Feminism? A Re-examination*. New York: Pantheon Books, 1986.
A collection of essays attempting to define feminism, examining the development of the contemporary feminist movement and theory, and considering the impact of a feminist perspective on specific areas such as medicine, the law, and women's work. Contributors include prominent feminist scholars, among them Mitchell and Oakley, Nancy Cott, Linda Gordon, and Judith Stacey. Editors' introduction traces social changes over the last decade and outlines the essays. Index.

Rowland, Robyn, ed. *Women Who Do and Women Who Don't Join the Women's Movement*. Boston: Routledge & Kegan Paul, 1984.
Women from the United States, Great Britain, Canada, and elsewhere explain why they do or do not identify themselves as feminists. Introduction by Rowland (a feminist) provides a social and political context and argues that, as a reaction to feminism, antifeminism is necessarily centered on similar issues. Contributors' statements about the women's movement are often highly personal and address a variety of issues—including abortion, work, fashion, language, and sexuality. Rowland's conclusion outlines "issues of contention," claiming that antifeminists emphasize differences between women and men and often distort feminists' aims.

Ethnic Identity and Racism

Allen, Paula Gunn. *The Sacred Hoop: Recovering the Feminine in American Indian Traditions*. Boston: Beacon Press, 1986.
  Essays by one of the country's most important Native American poets and critics. Allen addresses a wide range of topics—particularly issues connected to spiritual and mythical traditions in Native American culture, and writing by Native American women. Nevertheless, all the essays consider issues of ethnic identity and tradition, and many of them deal with specifically feminist topics. "Angry Women Are Building: Issues and Struggles Facing American Indian Women Today" and "Who Is Your Mother? Red Roots of White Feminism" address political movements and ethnic identity. Selected bibliography is divided into biographies and autobiographies, ethnologies and cultural analyses, and works of literature and criticism.

Bulkin, Elly, Minnie Bruce Pratt, and Barbara Smith. *Yours in Struggle: Three Feminist Perspectives on Anti-Semitism and Racism*. Brooklyn, N.Y.: Long Haul Press, 1984. Reprint. Ithaca, N.Y.: Firebrand Books, 1984.
  Individual essays by three women—one Jewish, one a white Southerner, and one black—exploring their experiences of racism and anti-Semitism. The essays form a kind of discussion among the three about the difficulties of confronting one's own prejudices. Pratt's is an especially moving effort to examine the attitudes with which she was reared. Includes list of useful organizations and other publications dealing with racism and anti-Semitism.

Davis, Angela Y. *Women, Race, and Class*. New York: Random House, 1981. Reprint. New York: Vintage Books, 1983.
  Davis, an important figure in the antiracist activism of the 1960's and 1970's, traces racism and class bias in American feminism from the abolition and suffrage movements to the present. She argues that early feminists placed women's rights before the rights of blacks and that contemporary white feminists continue to ignore black women's needs and, among other things, often invoke racist images of black men in discussions of rape.

Elsasser, Nan, Kyle Mackenzie, and Yvonne Tixier y Vigil. *Las Mujeres: Conversations from a Hispanic Community*. Old Westbury, N.Y.: Feminist Press, 1980.
  Oral histories of twenty-one Hispanic women living in New Mexico—some old enough to remember it as a Spanish-speaking territory. Participants discuss work, family, Hispanic culture, politics, and the effects of the area's cultural and economic changes.

Giddings, Paula. *When and Where I Enter: The Impact of Black Women on Race and Sex in America*. New York: William Morrow, 1984.

History of black women in the United States from slavery to the present, with particular emphasis on their political activism and the influence of black movements (such as those for abolition and civil rights) on white feminism. Giddings argues that "the progress of neither race nor womanhood" can proceed without black women. Chapters include discussions of the suffrage campaign, black feminist organizing, and the activism of the 1960's. Concludes with an analysis of the 1970's "failure of consensus," evident in the disorganized efforts of Shirley Chisholm's 1972 presidential campaign and white feminists' failure to recognize black women's key role in the ERA movement.

Hooks, Bell. *Ain't I a Woman: Black Women and Feminism*. Boston: South End Press, 1981.
Influential analysis of black women's position within and relationship to feminism. Hooks considers the experience of black women slaves, the historical devaluation of black women in the United States, the pervasive nature of sexism, and specific issues concerning black women and the contemporary women's movement (particularly racism within the movement). She analyzes black women's treatment by black men, white men, and white women, arguing that, whether positions have been defined in terms of race, class, or sex, black women have always ended up at the bottom of the hierarchy. Because of the impact of larger cultural systems of oppression, she sees the slave subculture as reproducing the gender hierarchy of the larger society and argues that black men in the modern Civil Rights movement continued to practice sexism, while white feminists have been guilty of racism. Nevertheless, she insists that feminism is meaningful for black women and defines herself and other black feminists as pioneers in a difficult struggle. Bibliography.

Hull, Gloria T., Patricia Bell Scott, and Barbara Smith, eds. *All the Women Are White, All the Blacks Are Men, But Some of Us Are Brave: Black Women's Studies*. Old Westbury, N.Y.: Feminist Press, 1982.
Introduction to feminist scholarship about black women. Essays by a variety of writers deal with racism in both educational institutions and scholarship and offer guidance to new approaches. Among the topics covered are black feminism, racism, and literature by and about black women. Includes several useful bibliographies and sample course syllabi from college courses.

Joseph, Gloria I., and Jill Lewis. *Common Differences: Conflicts in Black and White Feminist Perspectives*. Garden City, N.Y.: Doubleday, 1981.
Alternating essays by Joseph, who is black, and Lewis, who is white, discuss differences and similarities in the experiences of black and white women. Read together, the authors argue that feminists must acknowledge differences of race, class, and sexual orientation. Includes essays on racial conflicts in the women's movement and racism and sexism in media. Bibliography.

Lerner, Gerda, ed. "A Woman's Lot" and "Black Women Speak of Womanhood." In her *Black Women in White America: A Documentary History*. New York: Random House, 1972. Reprint. New York: Vintage Books, 1973.
Nineteenth and twentieth century documents dealing with black women's experience of sexism. Sections cover attitudes of both white and black men, sexuality, and black women as leaders. Includes writings by important historical and contemporary figures such as Sojourner Truth, Fannie Lou Hamer, and Shirley Chisholm.

Lorde, Audre. *Sister Outsider: Essays and Speeches*. Trumansburg, N.Y.: Crossing Press, 1984.
A collection of writings by a major black poet, on subjects from visiting Russia and Grenada to racism and poetry. Includes several well-known essays: "Poetry Is Not a Luxury," about women's need to imagine change; "Uses of the Erotic," distinguishing eroticism from pornography; and "The Master's Tools Will Never Dismantle the Master's House," which argues that it is impossible to fight oppression without challenging its basic premises and devising new ways of thinking and that fundamental change requires "learning how to take our differences and make them strengths."

Moraga, Cherríe, and Gloria Anzaldúa, eds. *This Bridge Called My Back: Writings by Radical Women of Color*. Watertown, Mass.: Persephone Press, 1981. Reprint. Latham, N.Y.: Kitchen Table/Women of Color Press, 1984.
Collection of essays, fiction, and poetry by black, Hispanic, Native American, and Asian-American women. Contributors examine their experiences of both racism and sexism in American culture, and they write about their ethnic, sexual, and class identities. Includes selected bibliography on Third World women in the United States.

Walker, Alice. *In Search of Our Mothers' Gardens: Womanist Prose*. San Diego: Harcourt Brace Jovanovich, 1983.
Collection of essays by the black American poet and novelist, author of *The Color Purple*. The collection's focus is Walker's experience as a black woman writer and feminist, particularly her search for literary role models and her discovery of early twentieth century black novelist and folklore collector Zora Neale Hurston. Includes an essay on her writing of *The Color Purple*.

Lesbian Issues

Beck, Evelyn Torton, ed. *Nice Jewish Girls: A Lesbian Anthology*. Trumansburg, N.Y.: Crossing Press, 1982.
Collection of essays and fiction on being both Jewish and lesbian. Contribu-

tions include discussions of anti-Semitism in the women's movement and antilesbian sentiment among Jews, reflections on the diversity of Jewish and lesbian experience, and the problems of being a Jewish feminist.

Cruikshank, Margaret, ed. *Lesbian Studies: Present and Future*. Old Westbury, N.Y.: Feminist Press, 1982.
Introduction to feminist scholarship about lesbians, including essays about experiences of scholars and teachers. The collection concentrates on issues related to teaching about lesbian issues but includes several useful bibliographic essays, sample course outlines, and guides to other resources.

Darty, Trudy, and Sandee Potter, eds. *Women-Identified Women*. Palo Alto, Calif.: Mayfield, 1984.
An anthology of essays on lesbians and lesbianism organized around the subjects of identity, oppression, and community. Writers such as Adrienne Rich, Paula Gunn Allen, and Melanie Kaye/Kantrowitz discuss coming out; lesbian relationships; the experiences of Native American and Puerto Rican lesbians; legal, health care, and work-related issues; and cultural topics such as poetry and music. Includes glossary, selected bibliography, and list of lesbian periodicals.

Eisenstein, Hester. "Lesbianism and the Woman-Identified Woman." In her *Contemporary Feminist Thought*. Boston: G. K. Hall, 1983.
Within a larger discussion and history of recent feminist theory, Eisenstein provides an outline of the development of lesbian-feminist theory from the early 1970's to the 1980's. She discusses the idea of lesbianism as an alternate definition of "true" womanhood, reactions to feminist lesbian-baiting, and lesbians' demands that heterosexuality—like sexism or capitalism—be examined as an institution.

Faderman, Lillian. *Surpassing the Love of Men: Romantic Friendship and Love Between Women from the Renaissance to the Present*. New York: William Morrow, 1981.
Faderman traces intimate emotional relationships between women over several centuries and discusses literary portrayals of these bonds. The book argues that such friendships were seen as part of normal female experience in the past, although Faderman does not identify all of her subjects as lesbians. A major contribution to the history of women whose most important relationships were with other women.

Raymond, Janice R. *A Passion for Friends: Toward a Philosophy of Female Affection*. Boston: Beacon Press, 1986.
Feminist history and analysis of female friendship, including but not limited to

lesbian relationships. Raymond emphasizes women's networks—including nuns and Chinese marriage resisters—as a means of resisting male domination. She outlines the traditional obstacles to women's friendship, among them popular assumptions about women's rivalry and the idea that women's most important relationships are necessarily with men, and argues that a vision of female friendship is necessary and central to achieving women's freedom.

Rich, Adrienne. "Compulsory Heterosexuality and Lesbian Existence." In *Powers of Desire: The Politics of Sexuality*, edited by Ann Snitow, Christine Stansell, and Sharon Thompson. New York: Monthly Review Press, 1983.
Controversial but influential essay arguing that male-dominated culture requires women to be heterosexual and that most women therefore see this as the "natural" choice. Rich recounts violent methods of enforcing women's heterosexuality and the ways that women find to resist it—including a range of bonds with other women, which she calls the "lesbian continuum." (Critics have argued that the idea of such a continuum threatens to erase the specific experience of women sexually identified as lesbians.)

_____ . *The Dream of a Common Language: Poems 1974-1977*. New York: W. W. Norton, 1978.
Poems by one of the leading American poets and one of the most influential lesbian writers. Includes "Twenty-One Love Poems," her best-known series of poems on lesbian sexuality.

Smith-Rosenberg, Carroll. "The Female World of Love and Ritual: Relations Between Women in Nineteenth-Century America." In her *Disorderly Conduct: Visions of Gender in Victorian America*. New York: Alfred A. Knopf, 1985.
Smith-Rosenberg argues that American women occupied a separate female sphere revolving around emotional support and practical aid. Separation from men and close ties to female friends and relatives allowed older women to pass on important skills to younger ones and made bonds among women central to their lives regardless of marital status. An extremely influential essay, based on extensive use of diaries, letters, and other personal writings from the period.

Wolf, Deborah Goleman. *The Lesbian Community*. Berkeley: University of California Press, 1979, rev. ed., with preface and afterword, 1980.
Field study of the San Francisco lesbian community, 1972 to 1975. Wolf traces the history of lesbian identity from early organizations such as the Daughters of Bilitis, emphasizing the importance of the present sense of community in contrast to past isolation, and the impact of feminism on lesbian identity. Includes chapter on lesbian mothers. Illustrations. Bibliography.

ECONOMICS

Women and Waged Work

Ascher, Carol, Louise DeSalvo, and Sara Ruddick, eds. *Between Women: Biographers, Novelists, Critics, Teachers, and Artists Write About Their Work on Women*. Boston: Beacon Press, 1984.
Personal essays emphasizing the authors' feeling of connection with their women subjects. Includes essays on studying Virginia Woolf's writing and Alice Walker's "Looking for Zora." Biographies of contributors and subjects. Illustrations.

Baxandall, Rosalyn, Linda Gordon, and Susan Reverby, eds. *America's Working Women: A Documentary History, 1600 to the Present*. New York: Random House, 1976.
Collection of writing on work by women from the early nineteenth century to 1975. The editors define "work" broadly and include subjects such as home manufacturing, industrialization, immigrants and migrant labor, unions, home-making, and war work. Illustrations.

Bergmann, Barbara R. *The Economic Emergence of Women*. New York: Basic Books, 1986.
Analysis of the changes wrought by women's greater participation in the American economy. Chapters address social changes, reasons for women's "emergence," gender differences in the workplace (including the wage gap, sex discrimination and affirmative action, and sex segregation), and effects on the family, the economy, the household, and national policy agendas. Bergmann argues that current changes represent a real alteration of centuries-old sex roles. She proposes new policies to reflect the new reality—including campaigns against discrimination and harassment, the enforcement of relevant laws and regulations, comparable worth, new child-care and child-support policies, and shifts in cultural attitudes—including a change in the number of hours considered a standard day's work. Tables, figures. Appendices summarize statistics and provide numerical analysis of labor market. Bibliography.

Degler, Carl. "Women's Work: The First Transformation," "Women at Work: Unions, Farms, and Professions," and "The Second Transformation in Women's Work." In his *At Odds: Women and the Family in America from the Revolution to the Present*. New York: Oxford University Press, 1980.
Historical essays describe the late nineteenth century and post-World War II "transformations" of women's work as women moved from home-based labor to wage-earning positions in the industrial and commercial sectors. Degler

argues that family duties shaped white women's relationship to work (less true for black women, who were more often compelled by economic necessity to work outside the home), that early labor unions excluded women and ignored their needs, and that World War II transformed the women's labor market.

Dudden, Faye E. *Serving Women: Household Services in Nineteenth-Century America*. Middletown, Conn.: Wesleyan University Press, 1983.
Dudden identifies two distinct forms of service: "help" or "hired girls," employed in household production, and "domestics," who were hired to work in an explicitly domestic capacity as household servants. She traces the nineteenth century transformation from "help" to "domestic," which she sees also as a move toward more demanding and more demeaning work, which meant in turn that fewer native-born women were willing to perform it. Chapters consider recruitment and hiring; ethnicity and race; urban and rural environments; issues of status; changes in ideas about motherhood, domestic work, and leisure; relations between employers and employees, including problems of "supervision." Includes many personal accounts and individual women's experiences, from both employers' and employees' perspectives. Includes list of manuscript sources.

Eisenstein, Sarah. *Give Us Bread But Give Us Roses: Working Women's Consciousness in the United States, 1890 to the First World War*. Boston: Routledge & Kegan Paul, 1983.
Examines the political and social consciousness of wage-earning women, focusing on the complexity of their responses to the dominant ideology. Eisenstein argues that working women critiqued their work environment, tensions between work and family life, and especially conflicts between their experiences and the period's conception of "womanly" behavior. Appendix includes historical documents (letters, speeches, leaflets) related to organizing efforts. Bibliography.

Farley, Lin. *Sexual Shakedown: Sexual Harassment of Women on the Job*. New York: McGraw-Hill, 1978.
A feminist review of the sexual harassment of women, from the history of the practice to contemporary examples. Includes discussion of the differences between harassment of white and black women and of women in traditional and nontraditional jobs. Farley also considers the impact of harassment on women's economic position (and vice versa), union policies, and civil treatment for victims of harassment. The analysis concludes with a call for affirmative action legislation and collective organizing by women against harassment.

Foner, Philip S. *Women and the American Labor Movement, from Colonial Times to the Eve of World War I*. New York: Free Press, 1979.

History of women's participation in the American labor movement as workers, activists and organizers, strikers, and the beneficiaries of changes in labor conditions. Includes discussions of specific strikes and organizations (among them, women's associations) and women in "women's" industries (such as the manufacture of women's clothing). The study emphasizes women's role as active participants, sharing concerns with men but also aware of their own issues. Illustrations. Extensive bibliography includes manuscript collections, unpublished sources, relevant newspapers, government and organizational documents and records.

Fox, Mary Frank, and Sharlene Hess-Biber. *Women at Work*. Palo Alto, Calif.: Mayfield, 1984
Introductory social science study of women and work in the United States. Provides a history from preindustrial to contemporary America, including discussions of World Wars I and II and the Depression. Chapters consider the impact of sex-role socialization and family relations; economic and legal issues; clerical and blue-collar jobs; professional and managerial occupations; minority women (focusing on black women but including Native American, Hispanic, and Asian American women); dual-worker families; and institutional perspectives on the future. The book emphasizes women's secondary status in the labor force, including sex segregation; changes in women's work roles and rate of participation in the world of paid work; the social and economic functions of work in our culture (including work's role in providing status and social contacts); and the biases of past studies centered on male workers' experiences. Tables and figures. Bibliography.

Gerson, Kathleen. "Women's Work and Family Decisions" and "Combining Work and Motherhood." In her *Hard Choices: How Women Decide About Work, Career, and Motherhood*. Berkeley: University of California Press, 1985.
Part of a study analyzing how structural changes in American society influence women's choices about motherhood and work. Chapters outline different attitudes toward work and family, suggest ways in which women accommodate their aspirations, and examine how women defined as "reluctant" mothers reconcile parenting and work.

Gold, Michael Evan. *A Dialogue on Comparable Worth*. Ithaca, N.Y.: ILR Press/ Cornell University, 1983.
A fictionalized dialogue on comparable worth—defined as the most important equal opportunity issue of the decade— providing a good introduction to both sides of the issue. An "advocate," "critic," and "moderator" discuss the wage gap, job evaluation plans, the social and economic consequences of comparable worth, laws, and the relationship of comparable worth to collective bargaining. The dialogue includes debates over the implications of particular legal

decisions and the concept of "intrinsic value" of jobs. Appendix includes reprints of pertinent legislation.

Gornick, Vivian. *Women in Science: Portraits from a World in Transition*. New York: Simon & Schuster, 1983.
An anecdotal examination of the experiences of women scientists, based on interviews with women of different ages and backgrounds and in a variety of fields (from ecology to physics). Gornick's account emphasizes both overt and covert discrimination against them, difficulties reconciling demands of career and family life, and her subjects' emotional investments in their professional work and in their identities as scientists.

Groneman, Carol, and Mary Beth Norton, eds. *"To Toil the Livelong Day": America's Women at Work, 1780-1980*. Ithaca, N.Y.: Cornell University Press, 1987.
Scholarly essays on the history of women and work. Contributions are grouped by historical period: 1780 to 1880 (including essays on labor activism and slave families), 1870 to 1920 (including studies of agricultural workers), 1910 to 1940 (including unions and domestic and other household workers), and 1940 to the late 1980's (including the Women's Bureau of the United Automobile Workers and Mexicana domestic workers). Many of the essays consider race and ethnicity and class issues. Editors' introduction identifies continuities across time (including the sexual division of labor and women's consistently lower wages relative to men's) and demonstrates how women's labor history alters both traditional labor history, which begins with men's experience, and women's history, which is focused on middle-class women. The editors define a continuum of paid and unpaid labor, arguing that women's work needs new models in order to be understood fully. Index.

Hewlett, Sylvia Ann. *A Lesser Life: The Myth of Women's Liberation in America*. New York: William Morrow, 1986.
Controversial book on contemporary conflicts between work and family life. Hewlett argues that feminism has actually weakened women's position by encouraging unrealistic career ambitions without providing the necessary social supports (maternity leave, quality child care, pay equity, and so on). Includes personal reflections by Hewlett on her experiences as a working mother.

Howe, Louise Kapp. *Pink-Collar Workers: Inside the World of Women's Work*. New York: G. P. Putnam's Sons, 1977.
Influential study of "pink collar" workers, women in traditionally female occupations—including beauticians, saleswomen, waitresses, and office workers—and one of first to look closely at such jobs. Howe takes an anecdotal approach to the subject, using personal accounts from interviews and observa-

tions of women workers. Appendix presents charts illustrating statistics on the female labor force.

Jones, Jacqueline. *Labor of Love, Labor of Sorrow: Black Women, Work, and the Family from Slavery to the Present*. New York: Basic Books, 1985.
Study of the history of black women and work, defining these women as both unique (because of their dual burden of race and gender discrimination) and representative of structural tensions in the American economy. Jones defines the black family as a site of struggle between black women, whose work and family responsibilities overlap, and whites who want to exploit their labor. She draws on archival records, documents, literature, and scholarly sources and traces the experiences of black women from the eighteenth century onward. Chapters on slavery, the Civil War and Reconstruction, the rural and urban South, migration to the North, the Depression, the 1940's and 1950's, and the civil rights movement and its aftermath. "Epilogue: 1984" describes the contemporary situation, including an exploration of the welfare state and the poverty of black female-headed families. Jones ends by calling for a "new moral vision of community," the integration of black women into the new political and economic system, and the coalition of black women and men and white women. Tables in appendices summarize statistics used in research. Illustrations. Selected bibliography includes citations of manuscript collections and unpublished work.

Kahn-Hut, Rachel, Arlene Kaplan Daniels, and Richard Colvard, eds. *Women and Work: Problems and Perspectives*. New York: Oxford University Press, 1982.
Collection of essays on women and work, focusing on issues of sex segregation and discrimination. Subjects range from nineteenth century attitudes to contemporary clerical work and a longitudinal study of organizational structures at American Telephone and Telegraph (AT&T). Sections—on the division of labor, home and market work, women's "invisible" contributions, and the "dual market"—all include essays on the origins of the particular problem, the current situation, and consequences and implications. Each essay is introduced by an abstract that suggests questions to consider while reading. Editors' conclusion identifies three feminist perspectives (liberal, Marxist, and radical) on women and work. Reference list and index.

Kaminer, Wendy. *Women Volunteering: The Pleasure, Pain, and Politics of Unpaid Work from 1830 to the Present*. Garden City, N.Y.: Anchor Press/Doubleday, 1984.
An examination of women's experience as volunteers and the meaning of that work. The book begins with a history of women volunteers, but most of it focuses on contemporary experience, drawing on interviews with a group of women committed to volunteer work. Kaminer asks why such women work

without pay and how they feel about it, considering their responses in the context of 1970's and 1980's attitudes about women and work. (She deals, for example, with the assumptions that volunteering is old-fashioned and with feminist critiques of women's voluntarism.) Interview subjects include those who volunteer full-time and those who combine volunteer and paid work; women who volunteer at a variety of jobs, including community and political organizations; a wide range of ages from college students to retirement; and women whose motivations vary from a desire to serve to a need to accommodate childrearing schedules.

Kanter, Rosabeth Moss. *Men and Women of the Corporation*. New York: Basic Books, 1977.
Major study of men and women in corporate culture, beginning from the premise that "jobs create people." The study is based on an extensive survey, interviews, group discussions, meetings, and observations of white-collar employees and office workers in a large multinational corporation. Chapters examine managers, secretaries, and corporate wives; work and organizational structures and processes; experiences of "token" women and men; and theoretical and practical implications of the research. Appendices describe methodology, data sources, and women's leadership in organizations (Kanter argues that leadership arises from the opportunity for power and a favorable position in the organization, not from psychological sex differences). Bibliography.

Keller, Evelyn Fox. *A Feeling for the Organism: The Life and Work of Barbara McClintock*. New York: W. H. Freeman, 1983.
Biography of geneticist Barbara McClintock, who developed the theory of genetic transposition, which transformed the way scientists conceived of genetic change. (McClintock won the Nobel Prize shortly after this book was published.) Keller emphasizes the difficulties McClintock faced as a woman scientist, particularly how her understanding of genetic behavior—based on a different attitude and approach to science—clashed with traditional views and led to her isolation from her colleagues. Includes an overview of genetic research, illustrations, and a glossary.

Kessler-Harris, Alice. *Out to Work: A History of Wage-Earning Women in the United States*. New York: Oxford University Press, 1982.
Examination of changes in women's work status, from Colonial limitations to women's twentieth century integration into the wage-labor force. Chapters focus on historical, economic, social, and technological changes and discuss the relationship between shifts in women's status in the workplace and in the family. Kessler-Harris, a major historian of women's work, emphasizes recent changes in the economy and the household and the subsequent recognition that wage-earning women are now the norm. Illustrations.

_____ . *Women Have Always Worked: A Historical Overview*. Old Westbury, N.Y.: Feminist Press, 1981.
The classic introduction to American women's work experience from Colonial
times to the present by one of the most important historians of American
women's work. Kessler-Harris argues that tension between the home and paid
labor spheres defines women's work experience. Includes discussions of wage
work, housework, the impact of World War II, and current sex discrimination.

Kirp, David L., Mark G. Yudof, and Marlene Strong Franks. "Gender Policy and
the Marketplace." In their *Gender Justice*. Chicago: University of Chicago
Press, 1986.
An analysis of gender issues in the workplace, including discussions of affirmative action, antidiscrimination policies, and comparable worth. The authors
critique both feminist and conservative theories, arguing that sex segregation
and the wage gap between men and women are created by both discrimination
and choice or decision making. They claim that men make "bigger human
capital investments" — for example, by finishing school or other training — and
put work first, while women often fit work around family concerns. The
chapter examines the potential of alternative schemes such as flex-time and
describes in detail a major discrimination suit against AT&T.

MacKinnon, Catharine A. *Sexual Harassment of Working Women: A Case of Sex
Discrimination*. New Haven, Conn.: Yale University Press, 1979.
One of the first sustained analyses of sexual harassment of women in the
workplace to argue that such harassment is a form of sex discrimination.
MacKinnon bases her complex argument on her view that two principles that
define discrimination operate simultaneously: Harassment is a practice that
expresses and reinforces women's inequality, and it occurs because the victim
is a woman. Chapters discuss inequities in women's status in the workplace
(including sex segregation and income inequities); the experience of sexual
harassment; specific cases with critiques of court decisions; the legal context;
and a theoretical analysis of sexual harassment as sex discrimination, including
an analysis of the relevant legal tradition. Appendices include applications of
the two approaches to sex discrimination and a legal brief on the subject.

Mattaei, Julie A. *An Economic History of Women in America: Women's Work, the
Sexual Division of Labor, and the Development of Capitalism*. New York:
Schocken Books, 1982.
Mattaei's aim is to uncover the effects on women of the development of
capitalism and the sexual division of labor (in which men and women perform
different and separate work), and this historical study is written from a
Marxist-feminist perspective. Sections address the Colonial family economy,
the cult of domesticity (in which the ideal woman was viewed as completely

separate from economic life), and the twentieth century breakdown of the sexual division of labor. Each section includes chapters on homemaking and married women, single and work-centered women, the development and workings of the sexual division of labor. The section on Colonial life includes a discussion of the impact of the slave economy, including the work of slave women. Tables.

Mclosh, Barbara. *"The Physician's Hand": Work Culture and Conflict in American Nursing.* Philadelphia: Temple University Press, 1982.
History of nursing from the 1920's to the 1970's, presented in terms of work culture—the distinct lore, social rules, and behavior associated with a particular kind of work or workplace—and with an emphasis on women's experience of work rather than the usual analysis of nursing, which focuses on professionalization. Melosh argues that nursing history is "the story of women workers' experience in a rationalizing service industry," and she includes chapters on the implications of professionalization, the history and culture of hospital schools, private-duty and public health nurses, and work in hospitals and other institutions. The conclusion describes recent changes, including the impact of feminism, with questions about the future of the field as nurses assume more responsibility and become identified as patient advocates.

Milkman, Ruth, ed. *Women, Work, and Protest: A Century of U.S. Women's Labor History.* Boston: Routledge & Kegan Paul, 1985.
Essays on women and labor organizing. Covers unions largely representing women (such as the Ladies' Garment Workers' Union and the Chicago Women's Trade Union League) and women's role in other unions (such as the Teamsters and the United Automobile Workers). Contributions include case studies of specific strikes and essays on larger issues in the history of women and unions; one essay deals with black women's efforts to organize. The collection emphasizes the intersection of gender and class consciousness and activism. Tables. Index.

Moore, Lynda L., ed. *Not as Far as You Think: The Realities of Working Women.* Lexington, Mass.: Lexington Books/D. C. Heath, 1986.
Essays on contemporary women and work, from social science analyses to anecdotal case studies. Contributors examine changing roles in the workplace, including discussions of women as bosses and managers; sex and work, including sexual harassment; how men and women approach conflict; balancing work and family; and dealing with work culture. The editor's introduction examines current views on women and work and surveys the problems women face—stressing social, moral, and economic reasons to seek solutions.

Newland, Kathleen. "Women Working" and "For Love or Money: Women's Wages." In her *The Sisterhood of Man.* New York: W. W. Norton, 1979.

These chapters discuss women's formal and informal participation in the worldwide labor force, unemployment among women, and issues related to women's income. The cross-cultural focus allows Newland to explore the broad range of women's work, from nomadic Iranian herders to Latin American industrial workers to professional and blue-collar workers in the United States. Information about women's income concentrates on industrialized countries and includes discussion of housework. Tables, figures.

Payne, Elizabeth Anne. *Reform, Labor, and Feminism: Margaret Dreier Robins and the Women's Trade Union League*. Urbana: University of Illinois Press, 1988.
A history of the Women's Trade Union League (WTUL), founded in 1903, and a biography of Margaret Dreier Robins (1868-1945), its president from 1907 to 1922. Payne sees the WTUL as a unique joining together of the labor and women's movements, one in which members—who ranged from unskilled workers to upper-class women—believed that women could come together across ethnic and class barriers to fight against social injustice. She analyzes the organization in the context of the Progressive Era's reform impulses. Bibliography includes manuscript collections, interviews, and other unpublished materials. Illustrations.

Ratner, Ronnie Steinberg, ed. *Equal Employment Policy for Women: Strategies for Implementation in the United States, Canada, and Western Europe*. Philadelphia: Temple University Press, 1978.
Papers on legislation, collective bargaining, and other policy-oriented strategies for achieving equal pay and widening employment opportunities for women. The collection includes studies comparing the status of women and men and discussions of legislation and other policies in individual countries. The editor summarizes themes and issues. Many contributors are current or former policymakers. Appendices on the contribution of labor market data and work analysis to the achievement of equality. Tables, figures, a bibliography, and an index.

Rosenfeld, Rachel Ann. *Farm Women: Work, Farm, and Family in the United States*. Chapel Hill: University of North Carolina Press, 1985.
Based on the 1980 Farm Women's Survey—the first comprehensive national survey of farm women—involving phone interviews with over twenty-five hundred farm women and more than five hundred men. Rosenfeld analyzes changes and trends in U.S. women's farm work in the context of the changing status of the family farm. Chapters analyze women's work and participation at home and on the farm; decision-making concerning home and farm; off-farm employment and division of labor (for example, who works off the farm and why); political and voluntary work; and farm women's attitudes toward their

roles. Conclusion emphasizes past definitions of farming as a male occupation and the importance of analyzing women's participation and roles, discusses variations among women, and cautions against making sweeping generalizations about farm women's experience. Tables and figures summarize interview responses. Appendix reproduces questionnaire from survey.

Ruddick, Sara, and Pamela Daniels, eds. Foreword by Adrienne Rich. *Working It Out: Twenty-three Women Writers, Artists, Scientists, and Scholars Talk About Their Lives and Work*. New York: Pantheon Books, 1977.
Personal essays by a variety of women exploring their experiences in the world of work. Contributors include scientist Evelyn Fox Keller, who writes on being a woman physicist; writer Alice Walker, who discusses the artistry of her mother's garden; and Tillie Olsen, who addresses the subject of women writers.

Sacks, Karen Brodkin, and Dorothy Remy, eds. *My Troubles Are Going to Have Trouble with Me: Everyday Trials and Triumphs of Women Workers*. New Brunswick, N.J.: Rutgers University Press, 1984.
Collection of essays on women and work grouped into sections on the family, technology, and the "global factory." Includes essays on the impact of technology, economic shifts, "de-skilling," race, sexual harassment, labor organizing, and domestic labor.

Schroedel, Jean Reith. *Alone in a Crowd: Women in the Trades Tell Their Stories*. Philadelphia: Temple University Press, 1985.
Personal narratives of twenty-five women in nontraditional blue-collar jobs. Addresses skilled trades, unskilled work, and union organizing. Sections cover the women's relationships to feminism, concerns about occupational safety and health, racial issues, unions, and family. Each section has short introduction. Index.

Statham, Anne, Eleanor Miller, and Hans O. Mauksch, eds. *The Worth of Women's Work: A Qualitative Synthesis*. Albany: State University of New York Press, 1987.
Collection of essays on women and work, ranging from women's approach to work, through specific types of work, to policy implications. Includes examinations of women's role as caretakers (domestic service in the family and waged work); as teachers, nurses, and social workers; and as workers in traditionally male positions, from factory work to management. Editors conclude, in "The Qualitative Approach to the Study of Women's Work: Different Method/ Different Knowledge," that a qualitative approach to gathering data puts the focus on the perspective of those studied, viewing them as active in constructing their own experience, instead of assuming the correctness of the dominant view. Indexes to names, concepts.

Stellman, Jeanne, and Mary Sue Henifin. *Office Work Can Be Dangerous to Your Health: A Handbook of Office Health and Safety Hazards and What You Can Do About Them.* New York: Pantheon Books, 1983.
A study of health risks to office workers (faulty or badly designed equipment, careless office design and furniture arrangement, inadequate safety provisions, and so on). Includes discussions of reproductive hazards and emphasizes employees' right to insist on a safe workplace. Appendices include a health and safety survey, a resource list, congressional testimony on office technology, model contract language, and a bibliography. Tables and illustrations.

Tavris, Carol, and Carole Offin. "Work: Opportunity, Power, and Tokenism." In their *The Longest War: Sex Differences in Perspective.* New York: Harcourt Brace Jovanovich, 1977, 2d ed. 1984.
Brief summary of research on women's position in the work force. The authors stress the interaction between coworkers' expectations and the behavior of working women and men (including the degree to which women workers live up to such expectations). They also discuss the failures of "feminine" organizational and management strategies and the effects of tokenism.

Treiman, Donald J., and Heidi I. Hartmann, eds. *Women, Work, and Wages: Equal Pay for Jobs of Equal Value.* Washington, D.C.: National Academy Press, 1981.
A National Research Council committee report on comparable worth, prepared for the U.S. Department of Labor and the Equal Employment Opportunity Commission. The study reviews pay differentials between male and female workers and issues involved in measuring the comparability of jobs (such as skill, effort, responsibility, tasks) in order to determine whether discrimination explains the wage gap. Includes discussions of the legal context (such as antidiscrimination legislation); evidence of differentials, including the effects of a variety of factors on pay rates; the relationship of the wage gap to institutional features of the job market; and approaches to overcoming discrimination through wage adjustments. The committee concludes that substantial pay discrimination exists, suggesting that job evaluation plans would provide helpful standards. The report includes a supplementary statement and a minority report by individual committee members. Tables and figures. Reference list.

Walshok, Mary Lindenstein. *Blue-Collar Women: Pioneers on the Male Frontier.* Garden City, N.Y.: Doubleday, 1981.
Examination of women breaking into and succeeding at skilled blue-collar occupations traditionally associated with men. Walshok asks how and why women seek blue-collar work—in context of family and personal history, home, previous work—and how on-job experiences affect other roles. She finds work to be central to their identities and deduces policy implications such as necessity of expanding girls' basic mechanical and other skills. Based on

study of eighty-seven California women. Includes extensive quotations from interviews. Appendix describes research methods.

Weiner, Lynn Y. *From Working Girl to Working Mother: The Female Labor Force in the United States, 1820-1980*. Chapel Hill: University of North Carolina Press, 1985.
A history of women and work in the United States, from the development of the idea of the "working girl" to the current controversies over working mothers. Weiner sees two distinct historical phases in the expansion of female labor (1820-1920 and 1920 to the present) and charts the changes in women's working lives that are reflected in the transition from a female work force characterized by single, self-supporting workers to one in which married women and mothers predominate. Individual chapters trace the development of attitudes toward women and work, including the relationship between working women and the social order, and examine topics such as immigration, working women's associations, and changing notions of motherhood and family relations. The conclusion argues that improved child-care and changes in American ideas about work will benefit not only working women but society as a whole. Tables, figures. Extensive bibliography, including manuscript sources and government publications.

Wertheimer, Barbara Mayer. *We Were There: The Story of Working Women in America*. New York: Pantheon Books, 1977.
A survey of the history of American women and work from the Colonial period to World War I. Wertheimer includes chapters on black women, unions and other labor organizations, factory work and trades, and women's work during the Civil War. Illustrations. Bibliography.

Wright, Barbara Drygulski, Myra Marx Ferree, Gail O. Mellow, Linda H. Lewis, Maria-Luz Daza Samper, Robert Asher, and Kathleen Claspell, eds. *Women, Work, and Technology: Transformations*. Ann Arbor: University of Michigan Press, 1987.
Interdisciplinary collection of original research and review essays on the impact on women of changes in work-related technology. Contributions range from historical discussions (including the advantages of the invention of the typewriter) to contemporary issues such as the reproductive hazards of new technology, changes in work processes, and the impact of computers. Other essays address computer equity for women, flight attendants' unions as examples of increasing militancy in the face of new technologies, and the impact of technology on farm workers. Wright's introduction rejects "technological determinism" (the idea that humans are limited in their potential responses to technology) and stresses the fact that technology, unlike science, must by definition acknowledge the social environment and the reactions of nonexperts. Index.

Women and Poverty

Bergmann, Barbara R. "Poverty and Single Parents." In her *The Economic Emergence of Women*. New York: Basic Books, 1986.
Chapter addresses the economic problems of women rearing children alone. Includes discussion of dependence on poverty-level assistance programs, lack of legal enforcement of child-support awards, and difficulty of juggling work and child-care responsibilities. Bergmann argues that women's greater participation in the work force has permitted an increase in the number of single mothers but that few such women actually earn enough to support their children comfortably. Includes analysis of the financial contributions (and their lack) from absent fathers and proposes new policies, such as unemployment insurance-type assistance, for single parents.

Buss, Fran Leeper, comp. *Dignity: Lower Income Women Tell of Their Lives and Struggles*. Introduction by Susan Contratto. Ann Arbor: University of Michigan Press, 1985.
A multiethnic oral history. Ten lower-income women describe their lives, from childhood onward. They discuss their experiences of work and poverty, puberty, childbirth, and family relationships. Brief introduction to each woman's story. Illustrations. Bibliography.

Byerly, Victoria. *Hard Times Cotton Mill Girls: Personal Histories of Womanhood and Poverty in the South*. Ithaca, N.Y.: ILR Press/Cornell University, 1986.
Oral histories of twenty Southern women recounting their experiences of work and poverty. The book is divided into sections dealing with changes in work and women's status, sexism, racism, and family. Includes a personal essay by Byerly on her return to the South and short introductions to each section. Illustrated.

Kozol, Jonathan. *Rachel and Her Children: Homeless Families in America*. New York: Crown, 1988.
Study of homeless women and children based on Kozol's personal interviews on the New York City streets and in shelters and other facilities. He examines the causes and effects of family homelessness, arguing that the main problem is a lack of affordable housing. Includes appendix suggesting possible solutions and list of relevant books and documents.

Lefkowitz, Rochelle, and Ann Withorn, eds. *For Crying Out Loud: Women and Poverty in the United States*. New York: Pilgrim Press, 1986.
Collection of articles, essays, and personal accounts about women and poverty. Sections are organized around the idea of the "feminization of poverty." Discussion of women's actual experience of poverty, their relationship to the

welfare system, and strategies for change. Each section introduced by editors. The collection emphasizes women's active agency (versus stereotypes of passive welfare recipients) and the variety of poor women's experiences. Includes Diana Pearce's influential "The Feminization of Poverty" and critiques of her view.

Levy, Frank. *Dollars and Dreams: The Changing American Income Distribution.* New York: Russell Sage Foundation, 1987.
An analysis of data collected in the 1980 U.S. Census, including many useful statistics and other information about women's economic status. The chapter "Households, Families, and the Government" describes changing patterns of households and family arrangements, including the rise in female-headed households and women and children living in poverty, and provides data on relative incomes of husbands and wives and economic inequality across and within families. Appendices describe the study's methodology, discuss the economic situation of the United States' Asian and Hispanic populations, and consider the effect of the underground economy. Tables, figures. Bibliography, name and subject indexes.

Pearce, Diana. "Farewell to Alms: Women's Fare Under Welfare." In *Women: A Feminist Perspective*, edited by Jo Freeman. 3d ed. Palo Alto, Calif.: Mayfield, 1984.
Briefly traces the origins of welfare for women and children from poorhouses and orphanages to the current Aid to Families with Dependent Children (AFDC) system. Pearce defines women's poverty as fundamentally different from men's because of the presence of their economically dependent children and gender handicaps in the workplace. She argues that the welfare system is based on a "male pauper model," with an emphasis on getting the recipient back into the workplace, and may be inappropriate for women with dependent children. Tables.

―――――――. "The Feminization of Poverty: Women, Work, and Welfare." In *For Crying Out Loud: Women and Poverty in the United States*, edited by Rochelle Lefkowitz and Ann Withorn. New York: Pilgrim Press, 1986.
The groundbreaking 1978 article that coined the phrase "feminization of poverty" to describe the increasing number of women (and children) living below the poverty line. Pearce discusses the decline in women's economic status, especially the impact of divorce on middle-class women, and criticizes the American welfare system for failing to assist women in the transition from assistance to participation in the work force. Tables.

Rodgers, Harrell R., Jr. *Poor Women, Poor Families: The Economic Plight of America's Female Headed Families.* Armonk, N.Y.: M. E. Sharpe, 1986.

Rodgers argues that changes in women's status and in families, without the appropriate adaptations of public policy, have led to the "feminization of poverty." He examines possible causes of the increase in female poverty, with a statistical overview by race, and reviews and critiques government policies of the 1970's and 1980's. The study compares European policies and concludes with a call for the reform of the U.S. welfare system, improved child-support and child-care systems, and greater government commitment to education. Tables and figures.

Rosen, Ellen Israel. *Bitter Choices: Blue-Collar Women in and out of Work*. Chicago: University of Chicago Press, 1987.
An extensive study of the job-loss experiences of married women and mothers working in New England mills and factories—"women with no public voice"—based on more than four hundred interviews. Rosen's focus is on how these women's lives are threatened by cutbacks, plant closings, and other job losses—reflections of the decline in U.S. manufacturing and the transformation of the global economy. Includes details of many individual women's day-to-day experience, examining how they deal with factory work, family life, job loss, and unemployment. Rosen argues that the loss of jobs and economic displacement affect women differently from men. Concludes with a call for a new social agenda, including federal assistance for displaced women workers. Appendix describes methodology.

Sheehan, Susan. *A Welfare Mother*. Introduction by Michael Harrington. Boston: Houghton Mifflin, 1976.
Portrait of a forty-three-year-old Puerto Rican mother of nine who lives on welfare in Brooklyn. Includes details of her history, family, financial situation, and experience with social service agencies—as well as a vivid depiction of her daily life. Originally written as a profile in *The New Yorker*, the book includes an afterword expanding on the history of the interview and responding to letters.

Shortridge, Kathleen. "Poverty Is a Woman's Problem." In *Women: A Feminist Perspective*, edited by Jo Freeman. 3d ed. Palo Alto, Calif.: Mayfield, 1984.
Discusses the predominance of women and children among the poor. Shortridge reviews statistics and offers social explanations to counter the myth of female dependence on husbands and fathers. She also proposes solutions, including preparing women for independent living. Figures.

_____ . "Working Poor Women." In *Women: A Feminist Perspective*, edited by Jo Freeman. Palo Alto, Calif.: Mayfield, 1975.
Surveys working poor women—including saleswomen, household workers, and agricultural workers. Describes their incomes, working conditions, and the

attitudes of employers. Discusses the economic mechanisms that devalue women's work, relevant legal factors (including "protective" legislation), and welfare. Proposals include negative income tax and political organizing by poor working women. Tables.

Sidel, Ruth. *Women and Children Last: The Plight of Poor Women in Affluent America.* New York: Viking Press, 1986.
Sidel uses interviews and empirical research to discuss both the "feminization of poverty" and the personal feelings of poor women. She argues that poor women often feel guilty and responsible for poverty that is actually the result of complex social and economic factors. The book proposes a national family policy, including women's access to employment, universal maternity leave, prenatal care, and day care.

Williams, Terry, and William Kornblum. *Growing Up Poor.* Lexington, Mass.: Lexington Books/D. C. Heath, 1985.
An ethnographic study of teenagers—largely black and Hispanic—growing up in poverty. Chapters examine teenage mothers, prostitution, work, and social habits and are based on teenagers' own accounts of their experiences.

HEALTH ISSUES AND SEXUALITY

Health and Health Care

Boston Women's Health Collective. *The New Our Bodies, Ourselves: A Book by and for Women*. New York: Simon & Schuster, 1984.
Updated version of the classic sourcebook on women's health. Written and compiled from a feminist and consumer-advocate perspective, it provides information on all areas of women's health, including sexuality, reproduction, and general health care. Tables, figures, charts, and illustrations.

Corea, Gena. *The Hidden Malpractice: How American Medicine Mistreats Women*. Boston: William Morrow, 1977. 2d ed., with afterword. New York: Harper Colophon, 1985.
Corea examines the male dominance of the American health-care system, from the historical exclusion of women from the medical professions to the widespread mistreatment of women's health problems. She proposes solutions through woman-controlled health care, but the updated edition argues that recent efforts by women to challenge the medical establishment have not reduced the malpractice or mistreatment of women patients. Appendix includes resource list.

Darty, Trudy, and Sandee Potter. "Lesbians and Contemporary Health Care Systems: Oppression and Opportunity." In their *Women-Identified Women*. Palo Alto, Calif.: Mayfield, 1984.
An attempt to redress the lack of attention to lesbian health care, emphasizing male control of the health-care system and the possibility of alternative care. The authors argue that lesbians face particular problems with traditional health-care delivery because of the system's heterosexual focus and insurers' refusal to see lesbian couples as families. They favor solutions through women-centered clinics and self-help.

Dreifus, Claudia. *Seizing Our Bodies: The Politics of Women's Health*. New York: Vintage Books, 1978.
A collection of essays on women and the health-care system, with sections on historical issues, reproduction, women medical professionals, and the women's health movement. Includes classic treatments such as Ellen Frankfort's "Vaginal Politics," about the impact of self-help women's clinics. Bibliography.

Ehrenreich, Barbara, and Deirdre English. *For Her Own Good: 150 Years of the Experts' Advice to Women*. Garden City, N.Y.: Anchor Press/Doubleday, 1979.

Popular and extremely influential feminist examination of the history of women and health care. Ehrenreich and English trace the professionalization of health care in the United States and doctors' usurpation of women's traditional healing skills. They argue that male "experts"—including medical professionals, media figures, and popular writers—have imposed their ideas about proper female behavior by mystifying health care. (More recent historical studies suggest that women may have been more actively involved in the medicalization of health care than the authors originally believed.)

Everywoman's Health: The Complete Guide to Body and Mind. 3d ed. Garden City, N.Y.: Doubleday, 1985.

Comprehensive handbook of women's health issues. Part 1, "Guide to Total Health," consists of essays on every aspect of women's health: physiological functions and systems; nutrition and weight; exercise; sexuality, contraception and abortion, pregnancy and childbirth, infertility, sexually transmitted diseases, and other gynecological problems; breast care; cosmetic surgery; alcohol and drug abuse; rape and spouse abuse; health on the job; mental and emotional health; roles across the life cycle; and health care and the health-care system. Part 2 is a detailed encyclopedia, presenting information in entry form. Appendices include suggested health exams and immunization guide for women, information on prescriptions, guide to health-care personnel, directory of health information (agencies, resources, and organizations). Illustrations, including color plates. Index.

Hubbard, Ruth, Mary Sue Henifin, and Barbara Fried, eds. *Biological Woman: The Convenient Myth.* Cambridge, Mass.: Schenkman, 1982.

Anthology of wide-ranging essays on women's sexuality, physiology, and health. Includes analyses of reproductive hazards in the workplace, sterilization abuse, women and menstruation, the displacement of female midwives by male physicians, and ideas for a course on black women's health. Extensive bibliography on "Women, Science, Health" gives comprehensive listing of work on issues ranging from evolution to eating disorders.

Morantz-Sanchez, Regina Markell. *Women Physicians in American Medicine: Sympathy and Science.* New York: Oxford University Press, 1985.

History of women medical practitioners from Colonial healers and midwives to the physicians of today, personalized through the extensive use of diary and letter excerpts. Morantz-Sanchez describes the emergence of formal medical education as part of women's nineteenth century move from the private into the public sphere. She emphasizes conflicts between the demands of family life and the demands of the profession, especially the scientific method and an ethos based on a male model. The book traces women doctors' early involvement in reform movements, their low visibility from 1930 to the 1960's, and their public resurgence alongside the feminism of the 1960's and 1970's. Appendix explains methodology. Bibliographic essay.

Rodriguez-Trias, Helen. "The Women's Health Movement: Women Take Power." In *Reforming Medicine: Lessons of the Last Quarter Century*, edited by Victor W. Sidel and Ruth Sidel. New York: Pantheon Books, 1984.
Rodriguez-Trias traces the development of a consumer-centered movement organized around women's health issues, arising in part out of the 1960's feminist consciousness-raising groups and women's dissatisfaction with traditional health care. The essay examines contraception and other reproductive-health issues, women in the health professions, and different perspectives of activists (some of whom focus on regulations, others on the reform of institutions, the development of alternative clinics, and so on).

Stage, Sarah. *Female Complaints: Lydia Pinkham and the Business of Women's Medicine*. New York: W. W. Norton, 1979.
The story of Lydia Pinkham (1819-1883) and her famous Vegetable Compound, a patent medicine sold for more than one hundred years as a cure for "female complaints" ranging from nerves to menstrual cramps and menopause. Stage sees the Compound as a social as well as a medical phenomenon, arguing that its popularity stemmed from women's reluctance to trust male gynecologists. The genius of Pinkham and her descendants, who ran the company after her death, lay in their ability to play on both the conventional view of women's "complaints" as excruciating and debilitating and their recognition of the inadequacies of professional medicine. Includes discussion of attempts by the Federal Drug Administration to regulate patent medicines. Illustrations.

Sexuality

Degler, Carl. "Women's Sexuality in Nineteenth-Century America." In his *At Odds: Women and the Family in America from the Revolution to the Present*. New York: Oxford University Press, 1980.
Historian Degler analyzes the popular notion that nineteenth century women were asexual. He argues that, though earlier advice books freely acknowledged female sexuality, many mid-century doctors and other writers denied it. He suggests that many women, including feminists, equated sexual restraint with personal autonomy and saw it as a means of controlling reproduction. The section includes "Organizing to Control Sexuality," describing women's participation in the Social Purity movement, which attempted to repress prostitution, drinking, and other "vices." The movement characterized men as lascivious and women as asexual, emphasizing women's control of male sexuality.

D'Emilio, John, and Estelle B. Freedman. *Intimate Matters: A History of Sexuality in America*. New York: Harper & Row, 1988.

A massive historical study tracing the meaning of sexuality in the United States. The book is organized into overlapping periods—1600-1800, 1780-1900, 1880-1930, and 1920-present—defined by changes in attitudes and policies on sexuality. The authors trace what they call "sexual meaning" from the initial preindustrial focus on family, marriage, and reproduction through twentieth century conflicts over notions of morality to contemporary "sexual liberalism." They address dominant ideas, crusades, and movements, emphasizing historical definitions of sexuality and of appropriate and inappropriate behavior. Includes analyses of changing institutions related to sexuality, such as marriage and prostitution, and of systems of sexual regulation—including the regulation of "deviance"—with an emphasis not simply on changing ideas about sexual behavior but also on the meanings of sexuality within culture. Considerable attention is given to media representations of sexuality and sexual behavior, gay and lesbian subcultures and liberation movements, questions of race (including racism, attitudes towards the sexuality of racial minorities), politics, and recent developments on abortion and acquired immuno-deficiency syndrome (AIDS). Illustrations.

Ehrenreich, Barbara, Elizabeth Hess, and Gloria Jacobs. *Remaking Love: The Feminization of Sexuality*. Garden City, N.Y.: Doubleday, 1986.

Discussion of the "sexual revolution" of the 1960's and 1970's, especially its impact on ideas about female sexuality and sexual behavior. The authors analyze mainstream changes in attitudes, the role of popular culture figures, the influence of serious studies, and pornography. *Remaking Love* differs from most analyses in its insistence that a *women's* sexual revolution actually occurred, fundamentally altering and expanding women's sexual potential.

Elia, Irene. *The Female Animal*. Introduction by Ashley Montague. New York: Henry Holt, 1988.

An introductory survey of females of all species, with an emphasis on sexual behavior and its role in evolution. Sections on mammals and primates are clearly sympathetic to sociobiology (the controversial theory that human behavior is genetically, not environmentally, based). Elia focuses on similarities between the sexual behavior of women and female animals, arguing for the evolutionary basis of modern human sexual, reproductive, and mothering behavior. Glossary. Extensive bibliography.

Faux, Marian. *Roe v. Wade: The Untold Story of the Landmark Supreme Court Decision That Made Abortion Legal*. New York: Macmillan, 1988.

Written from a pro-choice perspective, the book tells the story behind the 1973 Supreme Court decision overturning laws against abortion. Describes the case from its origins, when lawyers Linda Coffee and Sarah Weddington agreed to represent Norma McCorvey (the real "Jane Roe"), including its progress through the lower court, the appeal, and the Supreme Court hearings. Includes much personal detail, historical and political context. Illustrations.

Hite, Shere. *The Hite Report: A Nationwide Study of Female Sexuality*. New York: Macmillan, 1976.
Sections of this survey examine women's attitudes toward masturbation, orgasm, the "sexual revolution," lesbianism, and other aspects of female sexuality. Responses were garnered from open-ended questions about sexual behavior and relationships. The body of the text includes quotes and anecdotes drawn from the survey; appendices provide three versions of the questionnaire and statistical breakdowns.

Jay, Karla, and Allen Young. *The Gay Report*. New York: Summit Books, 1979.
Survey of sexuality among lesbians and gay men. The two groups are treated separately and answered separate questionnaires. The sections on lesbian sexuality include discussions of coming-out experiences, sexual behavior, self-image and socializing, relationships, lesbian role-playing, and (in the only section that deals with the two groups together) discrimination and liberation movements. Complete questionnaires included in text. Appendix includes profile of respondents.

Kinsey, Alfred, et al. *Sexual Behavior in the Human Female*. Philadelphia: W. B. Saunders, 1953.
Landmark study on female sexuality (the companion to one on male sexuality), based on a major statistical survey. Sections include responses to questions about preadolescent sexual development; marital, premarital, and extramarital behavior; and comparisons of men's and women's behavior. Includes explanation of methodology, data. Tables and figures.

Klaich, Dolores. *Woman + Woman: Attitudes Toward Lesbianism*. New York: Morrow Quill Paperbacks, 1979.
Study of lesbian sexuality and social experience, including a historical survey and chapters on Sappho, 1920's Parisian circles, Radclyffe Hall's *The Well of Loneliness*, the impact of Freudian theory, and the role of the gay liberation movement. Klaich uses interviews, anecdotes, and literature to argue against the traditional negative view of lesbianism. Selected bibliography.

Lorde, Audre. "Uses of the Erotic: The Erotic as Power." In her *Sister Outsider: Essays and Speeches*. Trumansburg, N.Y.: Crossing Press, 1984.
Black lesbian-feminist poet Audre Lorde argues against the suppression of eroticism, distinguishing it from pornography and claiming it as a source of creative energy and empowerment for women.

Rothman, Sheila M. "From the Nursery to the Bedroom." In her *Woman's Proper Place: A History of Changing Ideals and Practices, 1870 to the Present*. New York: Basic Books, 1978.
Rothman traces the shift, beginning in the 1920's, from a definition of the wife as primarily a mother to the notion of the wife as a romantic and sexual companion. Includes a discussion of Margaret Sanger's campaign for birth control and new ideas about child care.

Rubin, Gayle. "The Traffic in Women: Notes on the 'Political Economy' of Sex." In *Toward an Anthropology of Women*, edited by Rayna R. Reiter. New York: Monthly Review Press, 1975.
Highly influential essay on women's cultural function, kinship systems, and the "exchange of women" (the use of women to bind tribes and other kinship groups together through marriage ties). Rubin critiques Marxist and Freudian theories of women's role and proposes the "sex/gender system" as the best explanation for the complexity of women's position. Rubin was probably the first to argue, in this essay, that male-dominated society makes heterosexuality compulsory for women.

Rubin, Lillian Breslow. "Blue-Collar Marriage and the Sexual Revolution." In *Family in Transition: Rethinking Marriage, Sexuality, Child Rearing, and Family Organization*, edited by Arlene S. Skolnick and Jerome H. Skolnick. 5th ed. Boston: Little, Brown, 1986.
This essay (excerpted from Rubin's larger study of working-class families) examines attitudes toward sexuality among working-class husbands and wives. She emphasizes differences in their expectations, limitations on acceptable sexual behavior, and the extent to which the wives she interviewed perceive their sexuality as defined by and existing for their husbands. Includes quotations from interview subjects.

Smith-Rosenberg, Carroll. "From Puberty to Menopause: The Cycle of Femininity in Nineteenth-Century America." In her *Disorderly Conduct: Visions of Gender in Victorian America*. New York: Alfred A. Knopf, 1985.
Based on professional and popular writings by doctors. Smith-Rosenberg argues that nineteenth century physicians saw women as dominated by their reproductive organs. She describes attitudes toward menstruation, female sexuality, and menopause as reinforcing a view of women as physically weak and unstable and justifying the perpetuation of traditional roles.

Snitow, Ann, Christine Stansell, and Sharon Thompson, eds. *Powers of Desire: The Politics of Sexuality*. New York: Monthly Review Press, 1983.
A collection of writings on sexuality, covering issues such as nineteenth century sexual morality, lesbian and gay GI's, sex research, pornography, and the

importance of sexuality in feminist theory and politics. Includes Adrienne Rich's "Compulsory Heterosexuality and Lesbian Existence."

Stanley, Julia Penelope, and Susan J. Wolfe, eds. *The Coming Out Stories*. Foreword by Adrienne Rich. Watertown, Mass.: Persephone Press, 1980.
Poems, journal entries, letters, essays, and stories about coming out as a lesbian. Includes essays by writers Minnie Bruce Pratt and Joanna Russ, who describes her longtime refusal to acknowledge her sexual identity.

Stimpson, Catherine R., and Ethel Spector Person, eds. *Women: Sex and Sexuality*. Chicago: University of Chicago Press, 1980.
Collection of scholarly feminist essays on women and sexuality. The book includes some especially useful review essays surveying scholarship and research on the connections among biology, sex, and gender; pregnancy; sexuality and maternity. Index.

Tavris, Carol, and Carole Offin. "Sexuality." In their *The Longest War: Sex Differences in Perspective*. New York: Harcourt Brace Jovanovich, 1977. Reprint. 1984.
This chapter briefly traces attitudes toward sexuality from the Victorian period through *The Kinsey Report*, William Masters' and Virginia Johnson's studies, and more recent controversies over female sexuality. It emphasizes cultural influences on sexual rules, as opposed to innate differences in male and female behavior.

Vance, Carol S., ed. *Pleasure and Danger: Exploring Female Sexuality*. Boston: Routledge & Kegan Paul, 1984.
Papers—including some poems and short stories—presented at a 1982 Barnard College conference, "Towards a Politics of Sexuality." Contents cover topics such as sexuality and feminism, lesbian role-playing, children and sexuality, and popular sex literature. Also included is a discussion of the controversy (largely over issues about lesbian sexuality) that surrounded the conference.

Reproductive Issues

Birth Control and Abortion
Callahan, Sidney, and Daniel Callahan, eds. *Abortion: Understanding Differences*. New York: Plenum, 1984.
Essays on abortion and ethics, edited by an antiabortion wife and pro-choice husband. Contributors include sociologists, political scientists, medical ethi-

cists, and theologians—most of whom were reared as Catholics. The collection encompasses the full range of pro-choice and antiabortion views, including some writers who simultaneously oppose both the absolute right to and the absolute prohibition of abortion. Essays consider policy implications of poll data on abortion, the relationship between abortion and debates over the meaning of life and definitions of personhood, and questions of equality and women's rights. Most are followed by a "commentary" (response and critique) focusing on philosophical, ethical, and epistemological issues.

Collins, Carol C., ed. *Abortion: The Continuing Controversy.* New York: Facts on File, 1984.
Facsimile reprints of editorials and editorial cartoons on all sides of the abortion question. The introduction covers abortion and public opinion. The contents are grouped into selections on Supreme Court decisions, politics (including religion, violence at clinics), government funding, and abortion, pregnancy, and family planning. All sections have short introductions. Index.

Degler, Carl. "Limiting Fertility." In his *At Odds: Women and the Family in America from the Revolution to the Present.* New York: Oxford University Press, 1980.
Degler discusses nineteenth century uses of and attitudes toward contraception. He notes that, despite ignorance of the details of ovulation, many doctors gave very specific advice about birth control. The chapter "Abortion: Women's Last Resort" examines the sudden increase in the abortion rate in the 1830's and 1840's, changing social and legal attitudes, and the rise of organized opposition among physicians and others.

Francke, Linda Bird. *The Ambivalence of Abortion.* New York: Random House, 1978. Reprint. Laurel Books/Dell Books, 1982.
First-person accounts of abortion experience written from pro-choice perspective but focusing on a wide range of emotional reactions, from guilt to relief. The introduction describes Francke's own experience in an essay originally published anonymously; the text includes the history of abortion and related laws and descriptions of standard procedures. The study is based on interviews with single and married women, men, couples, adults, teenagers, and parents. It describes experiences both pre- and post-1973, when the *Roe v. Wade* decision legalized abortion, including a chapter on the abortion underground over the last fifty years and women's experiences of illegal abortion. The concluding chapter analyzes current political threats to abortion rights.

Gordon, Linda. *Woman's Body, Woman's Right: A Social History of Birth Control in America.* New York: Viking Press, 1976.
The first comprehensive history of birth control in the United States. Gordon

identifies three major phases in the movement, each expressing the interests of different groups of women: the "voluntary motherhood" of late nineteenth century feminism; the development of separate contraception-oriented organizations, from 1910 to 1920; and the liberal, reform-centered "planned parenthood" stage, from the 1940's onward. She examines controversies over contraception, population control, and abortion and argues that reproductive freedom is central to women's freedom.

Harrison, Beverly Wildung. *Our Right to Choose: Toward a New Ethic of Abortion.* Boston: Beacon Press, 1983.
An analysis of abortion by a pro-choice feminist ethicist-theologian, emphasizing the intimate connections between politics and morality. Harrison argues for abortion in terms of the "social good" of women's right to control reproduction, distinguishing between "moral" and social-science analyses of issues. Chapters include reevaluations of the history of abortion (reconceptualizing Christian attitudes, "notes" toward a feminist perspective) and the debate on fetal life. A relatively sophisticated philosophical argument is made accessible by explanations throughout of issues, terms, and the history of specific controversies.

Hartmann, Betsy. *Reproductive Rights and Wrongs: The Global Politics of Population Control and Contraceptive Choice.* New York: Harper & Row, 1987.
An analysis of international issues surrounding population control and reproduction, emphasizing the importance of choice and "the inviolability of individual reproductive rights." Hartmann argues that, since improved living conditions and changes in the position of women lead to smaller families, basic social and economic changes in developing countries will reduce population problems and eliminate the need for the Western imposition of technology-oriented solutions. Individual chapters examine international organizations promoting population control and controversies over various methods of contraception. Appendix lists organizations involved in global reproductive issues.

Luker, Kristin. *Abortion and the Politics of Motherhood.* Berkeley: University of California Press, 1984.
Detailed study of the pro-choice and antiabortion movements, beginning with the history of the issue in the United States. Luker traces the emergence of abortion as the subject of political debate and the development of oppositional movements; analyzes the worldviews and commitments of activists on both sides; and positions pro-choice and antiabortion stances in larger political, philosophical, and religious contexts. Using historical sources and lengthy quotations from personal interviews with activists, she argues that the two sides share no assumptions and that deeply involved activists oversimplify public opinion. Appendix explains methodology. Tables. Bibliography.

McDonnell, Kathleen. *Not an Easy Choice: A Feminist Re-examines Abortion.* Boston: South End Press, 1984.
McDonnell, a Canadian feminist, reconsiders abortion rights (and remains pro-choice) in the light of her own ambivalence and the feminist insistence on the importance of basing political theories on personal experiences and reactions. Chapters examine women's experience of abortion, men's attitudes, issues of morality, definitions of "choice," the development of the antiabortion movement, and various ways of controlling reproduction. Bibliography.

Messer, Ellen, and Kathryn E. May. *Back Rooms: Voices from the Illegal Abortion Era.* Foreword by Marge Piercy. New York: St. Martin's Press, 1988.
Personal accounts of the experience of illegal abortion from the 1940's to the 1973 *Roe v. Wade* Supreme Court decision. All are presented from a pro-choice perspective. Voices include both women and men (both those involved in the pregnancy and pro-choice activists), as well as doctors who performed illegal abortions. Accounts describe the circumstances of the abortions, physical risks, legal dangers, and the struggle to change the laws.

Petchesky, Rosalind Pollack. *Abortion and Woman's Choice: The State, Sexuality, and Reproductive Freedom.* Boston: Northeastern University Press, 1985.
Petchesky argues that reproduction and fertility control are historically determined and socially organized, and that it therefore requires historical and social perspective to explain the great differences in women's experiences. The introduction outlines the origins and theoretical implications of the feminist stance on abortion. The book is divided into sections tracing the history of attitudes, demographics, related movements (including eugenics), medical responses, and legislation; recent trends, class and race differences, poor women's access to abortion, politics, and inadequacies of contraceptive techniques; and antiabortion/New Right movements and court decisions. Argues that no individual solutions to the abortion question exist because choices about reproductive politics depend on social conditions.

Pogrebin, Letty Cottin. "The Politics of Pregnancy and Motherhood." In her *Family Politics: Love and Power on an Intimate Frontier.* New York: McGraw-Hill, 1983.
Pogrebin argues that the right to abortion—and thus to woman-controlled mothering—is the key to genuine respect for motherhood. The chapter looks at the antiabortion movement within the context of the battle for the control of women as mothers.

Reardon, David C. *Aborted Women: Silent No More.* Chicago: Loyola University Press, 1987.

An antiabortion analysis of the physical and emotional trauma following the procedure ("Post-Abortion Syndrome"), based on a survey conducted through chapters of an antiabortion organization. Among women reporting on their abortion experiences, pro-choice advocates and antiabortionists, feminists, rape victims, and women who experienced legal and illegal abortions are profiled. Chapters consider the impact of the abortion experience on later children and abortion as business. Appendix provides survey and results. Foreword by member of Women Exploited by Abortion, who describes her own experience.

Reed, James. *From Private Vice to Public Virtue: The Birth Control Movement and American Society Since 1830*. New York: Basic Books, 1978.
A history of the birth-control movement, including the development of contraceptive technology. Emphasis on social changes and shifts in values and medical attitudes. Several sections focus on the role of major figures— Margaret Sanger, Robert L. Dickinson, and Clarence J. Gamble among them. The study includes a discussion of American fears of both depopulation and overpopulation, a history of definitions and functions of the family, and a long section on the development of the birth-control pill. Reed argues that birth control was promoted and supported mainly by women (who saw it as the only route to greater control over their lives), medical professionals, and those worried about eugenics but did not garner enough support from the American public to result in a U.S. government policy. He argues that real "family planning" has not yet been tried seriously in the United States or elsewhere. Illustrations. Bibliographic essay.

Sachdev, Paul, ed. *International Handbook on Abortion*. Westport, Conn.: Greenwood Press, 1988.
Essays about abortion around the world, including industrialized countries (both in the West and in the Eastern Bloc) and countries of the Third World. Individual essays discuss the history of the development of abortion policy, its current legal status, popular and cultural attitudes, demographics of women having abortions (including statistics on contraceptive use, adolescents, and repeat abortions), research, illegal abortions, and the relationship between abortion and other forms of fertility regulation. References for each country. Editor's introductory essay reviews international trends and draws some generalizations about the impact of legislation on abortion rates and the relation of abortion to changes in fertility rates. Provides an overview of abortion laws around the world. Tables and figures.

Sanger, Margaret. *An Autobiography*. New York: W. W. Norton, 1938. Reprint. New York: Dover Publications, 1971.
Memoirs of the American birth-control pioneer and activist (1879-1966), from

her childhood to her successful 1930's campaign to distribute contraceptive information. Includes descriptions of her arrest and conviction for dispensing illegal advice, discussion of the campaign to change the laws prohibiting the dispensing of contraceptive information and devices, and an account of her travels.

Shapiro, Howard. *The New Birth-Control Book: A Complete Guide for Women and Men*. Englewood Cliffs, N.J.: Prentice-Hall, 1988.
A question-answer format provides information on reproduction, birth-control methods, abortion, and sterilization. Includes considerations of male contra-ceptives, including vasectomy, and detailed descriptions of all methods—their effectiveness, advantages, and disadvantages. Illustrations and figures.

Smith-Rosenberg, Carroll. "The Abortion Movement and the AMA, 1850-1880." In her *Disorderly Conduct: Visions of Gender in Victorian America*. New York: Alfred A. Knopf, 1985.
This essay traces the emergence of the political controversy over abortion in mid-nineteenth century America. Smith-Rosenberg discusses the role of the American Medical Association in lobbying for laws governing abortion (pre-viously legal during the first trimester) and how the antiabortion movement played into popular conceptions of "True Womanhood" and existing conflicts between doctors and medical reformers.

Pregnancy and Childbirth

Arms, Suzanne. *Immaculate Deception: A New Look at Women and Childbirth*. Boston: Houghton Mifflin, 1975. Reprint. New York: Bantam Books, 1977.
A critique of the traditional view of childbirth as a disease needing medical intervention, promoting the naturalness of the experience and the possibility of women controlling the process. Arms includes descriptions of births, discus-sions and critiques of procedures arranged for the convenience of medical personnel, the use of drugs during delivery, and unnecessary and routine medical intervention. Includes quotes from women, doctors, nurses, and mid-wives; several chapters discuss midwives, home births, and prosecutions for illegal deliveries. Illustrations and tables.

Ashford, Janet Isaacs, ed. *Birth Stories: The Experience Remembered*. Tru-mansburg, N.Y.: Crossing Press, 1984.
Anthology of personal narratives and poems describing birth experiences in the United States and Canada from 1915 to 1983. (Most are by women and describe the experience of delivery, but some are by men or other observers.) Selections cover a wide range of experiences, methods, and contexts—including still-births and adoption. Editor's introduction discusses the importance of a "good" birth experience and includes statistics comparing the births described

in the anthology to national averages for intervention, mortality, and other variables. Includes glossary and notes explaining, correcting, and expanding accounts. Illustrations.

Leavitt, Judith Walzer. *Brought to Bed: Childbearing in America, 1750-1950*. New York: Oxford University Press, 1986.

A comprehensive history of childbirth, arguing that the experience remained controlled by and centered on women until it moved from the home to the hospital, but that women participated in and even welcomed the medicalization of childbirth. Chapters trace the development of obstetrics practiced by male physicians and the introduction of forceps and anesthesia. Draws heavily on diaries, letters, and other personal texts. Leavitt emphasizes historical reliance on women friends and relatives and the bond created by shared experience. Includes "Chronology of Events in Childbirth History," glossary of relevant medical terms. Illustrations.

McKaughan, Molly. "Our Real Biological Clocks," "Getting Pregnant: Fertility and the Clock," "The Elderly Primagravida," and "Nurturing Comes Naturally." In her *The Biological Clock: Reconciling Careers and Motherhood in the 1980s*. New York: Doubleday, 1987.

Within a larger survey of women who postponed childbearing, chapters discuss basic biological considerations, from mechanisms of reproduction and fertility problems to risks for older women having a first child ("elderly primagravida") and questions of an innate "maternal instinct." Personal accounts from survey subjects describe the impact of a "biological clock" on their decisions. The chapter on nurturing argues that women are natural nurturers and that men and women are distinguished by a "separate hormonal heritage."

Petchesky, Rosalind Pollack. "Foetal Images: The Power of Visual Culture in the Politics of Reproduction." In *Reproductive Technologies: Gender, Motherhood, and Medicine*, edited by Michelle Stanworth. Minneapolis: University of Minnesota Press, 1988.

Petchesky examines the impact of technological developments that allow people to see images of the fetus. She analyzes the use of fetal images in the controversial antiabortion film "The Silent Scream" and the effects of ultrasound images on women's feelings about pregnancy, suggesting that such images may speed a woman's "bonding" with the fetus.

Sorel, Nancy Caldwell, ed. *Ever Since Eve: Personal Reflections on Childbirth*. New York: Oxford University Press, 1984.

A wide-ranging collection of excerpts describing childbirth, from Napoleon and Queen Victoria to "I Love Lucy" and Maya Angelou. Both men (Sigmund Freud, Pablo Picasso, Leo Tolstoy, Malcolm X, Elie Wiesel) and women (Margaret Mead, Golda Meir, Ingrid Bergman) describe the experience or observation of birth. Includes fictional and nonfictional, contemporary and historical accounts, with cross-cultural examples from around the world. The anthology begins with a description of the editor's experience and ends with descriptions of two other contemporary births, one at home. Sections cover theories about conception, pregnancy, and birth (ranging from traditional cultures' ideas to psychoanalytic theory); fathering, twins, politics, stillbirths, and miscarriages.

Wertz, Richard W., and Dorothy C. Wertz. *Lying-In: A History of Childbirth in America*. New York: Free Press, 1977.
History of childbirth in the United States from Colonial times to the late 1970's, describing the shift in its identification from a social event aided by women to a medical event involving doctors. The Wertzes describe American birth as unique in being routinely defined as a disease needing medical intervention and discuss social, cultural, and medical aspects as interacting processes. A chapter on government involvement in financial and legal spheres describes policies—including a campaign against midwives—as developing out of child-welfare movements, the growth of professional philanthropy, and the need to improve health care for poor women and children. The authors conclude that the American medicalization of childbirth is probably rooted in seventeenth century Protestantism, and they argue that the country needs a detailed national policy, including the encouragement of nurse-midwifery and maternity leaves. Illustrations. Bibliography.

Infertility, Reproductive Technology, and Related Issues
Arditti, Rita, Renate Duelli Klein, and Shelley Minden, eds. *Test-Tube Women: What Future for Motherhood?* Boston: Pandora Press, 1984.
Collection of essays critiquing the impact on women of the new reproductive technologies. Contributors examine *in vitro* fertilization, embryo transplants, surrogacy, sterilization abuse in Third World countries, abortion, and non-technological alternatives, emphasizing the necessity for women to take control of reproduction. Several essays deal with ethical issues, including the implications of reproductive technology for the rights of the disabled. Includes Rayna Rapp's personal essay "XYLO: A True Story," about her abortion of a Down's syndrome fetus following amniocentesis. Glossary, resource list, and bibliography.

Chesler, Phyllis. *The Sacred Bond: The Legacy of Baby M*. New York: Times Books, 1988.
Examination of the Mary Beth Whitehead/"Baby M" surrogacy case, with discussions of the issues surrounding surrogate mothering. The book follows the case through the final verdict, including a journal of Chesler's activism on Whitehead's behalf and against legal surrogacy. She examines attitudes about

motherhood, comparing the Whitehead-Stern custody fight to normal post-divorce custody battles. Appendices include the original surrogacy agreement between Whitehead and William Stern and a variety of court documents.

Corea, Gena, Renate Duelli Klein, Jalna Hanmer, Helen B. Holmes, Betty Hoskins, Madhu Kishwar, Janice Raymond, Robyn Rowland, and Roberta Steinbacher. *Man-Made Women: How New Reproductive Technologies Affect Women*. London: Hutchinson, 1985.
Collection of essays written from a feminist antireproductive technology perspective. Analyzes a wide range of technologies, including superovulation, ova recovery, and embryo transfer. Argues that the new technologies mean a new victimization of women, especially "previctimization" through *in utero* sex selection. Essays emphasize the new technologies' potential for the manipulation of women's reproductive function and the necessity of questioning even apparently positive aspects of reproductive technology (such as the "benefits" to infertile women). Corea's "The Reproductive Brothel" suggests the possibility of selling women's reproductive services in a manner analogous to the business of prostitution. Each essay includes a bibliography.

Menning, Barbara Eck. *Infertility: A Guide for the Childless Couple*. Englewood Cliffs, N.J.: Prentice-Hall, 1977, 2d ed. 1988.
Menning explores the medical and "psychosocial" aspects of infertility, offering explanations for and possible ways of coping with it. The guide provides basic information about common causes, standard medical procedures, new reproductive technologies, and alternative solutions (including adoption and surrogacy). Examines the impact of infertility on marriage, personal identity, and sexuality. Includes glossary, bibliography, and resource list.

Stanworth, Michelle, ed. *Reproductive Technologies: Gender, Motherhood and Medicine*. Minneapolis: University of Minnesota Press, 1988.
A collection of essays about the issues raised by new developments in reproductive technology. The contributors emphasize the complexity of the problems, the implications for notions of motherhood, and new legal issues (such as definitions of and questions about paternity). Essays are written from a feminist perspective but question some feminist fears, such as the implications of genetic screening for the sex of the fetus. Includes discussions of *in vitro* fertilization, surrogacy, and artificial insemination.

Other Health Issues

Banner, Lois W. *American Beauty*. Chicago: University of Chicago Press, 1983.
Study of personal beauty in the United States from the Colonial period to the

modern age, emphasizing American culture's identification of its pursuit as part of women's role. Banner traces the development of the cultural ideal and its commercialization through festivals, beauty contests, and consumer items; changes in fashionable body images, including their association with actresses and other figures of popular culture; and the impact of class and the women's movement on notions of beauty and fashion. Illustrations. Selected bibliography.

Bruch, Hilde. *The Golden Cage: The Enigma of Anorexia Nervosa.* Cambridge, Mass.: Harvard University Press, 1978. Reprint. New York: Vintage Books, 1979.
An examination of the causes, stages, physical effects, and treatment of anorexia. Bruch emphasizes the psychological origins of the disease and the distortion of body image, arguing that anorectics' need to be "perfect"— especially to please and protect their mothers—leads them to make unreasonable demands on themselves and to see starvation as an achievement and an exertion of self-control.

Brumberg, Joan Jacobs. *Fasting Girls: The Emergence of Anorexia Nervosa as a Modern Disease.* Cambridge, Mass.: Harvard University Press, 1988.
Study of the development of anorexia nervosa as a specific disease, distinct from earlier forms of self-starvation (such as "anorexia mirabilis," or food refusal associated with female saints). Focusing on the rise of anorexia (and, to a lesser extent, bulimia) in the nineteenth and twentieth centuries, Brumberg disputes theories that anorexia resulted primarily from either a culturally imposed ideal of female thinness or adolescent girls' refusal of adult sexuality. She argues instead that it represents a complex response to the intersection of cultural messages about food (including the equation of food with love), family life, body image, and particular aspects of women's roles (for instance, the nineteenth century focus on marriage as an occupation for middle-class girls). Afterword concentrates on the post-1960's recurrence, suggesting that it results from a rapid "social change in the realm of food and sexuality." Illustrations.

Chavkin, Wendy, ed. *Double Exposure: Women's Health Hazards on the Job and at Home.* New York: Monthly Review Press, 1984.
Essays cover a wide range of work-related health risks in a variety of workplaces—including the electronics industry, nursing, office work, and migrant agriculture—and risks associated with the home, such as pollutants. Among topics addressed are reproductive risks for women and men, grassroots and union organizing to protect women on the job, effects of stress and sexual harassment on health, and health hazards for minority women. Illustrations.

Deegan, Mary Jo, and Nancy A. Brooks, eds. *Women and Disability: A Double Handicap*. New Brunswick, N.J.: Transaction Books, 1985.

An anthology of essays on women and disabilities, ranging from general topics (such as insurance benefits, the effects of sexism) to discussions of specific disabilities (such as chronic renal failure, visual impairment). Includes essays written from economic and social perspectives, some emphasizing the self-help movement. The editors' introduction argues that disabled women find it especially difficult to be assertive in the face of stereotypes and sexism. Tables and brief abstracts of each article.

Delaney, Janice, Mary Jane Lupton, and Emily Toth. *The Curse: A Cultural History of Menstruation*. New York: New American Library, 1976. Rev. ed. Urbana: University of Illinois Press, 1988.

Examination and critique of cultural attitudes toward menstruation, particularly taboos. *The Curse* attempts to demystify menstruation and emphasize the bond among women through an analysis of religious and medical views (including psychoanalysis), physiological process, cultural and symbolic significance, and the presentation of menstruation in advertising. Includes a chapter on premenstrual syndrome, a section on menopause, and a discussion of literary images. The afterword of the revised edition updates each chapter.

McConville, Brigid. *Women Under the Influence: Alcohol and Its Impact*. New York: Schocken Books, 1985.

An introductory examination of women and alcoholism, beginning with personal accounts by women alcoholics. The focus is on physical effects, and the book includes descriptions of symptoms, self-check lists, and questions. Included is a brief discussion of the social context, images of women drinkers, and the political significance of women's alcoholism. Figures. Although based on British sources and interviews, the book includes a list of useful addresses in the United States.

Orbach, Susie. *Hunger Strike: The Anorectic's Struggle as a Metaphor for Our Age*. New York: W. W. Norton, 1986.

Orbach, an important writer on women's health issues, argues that anorexia represents both a rebellion against and an accommodation to women's social roles. She criticizes current treatment programs that associate anorexia with the refusal to become an adult and likens standard treatment of anorexia to the nineteenth century "rest cure" for hysterics. Proposes self-help programs that address patients' feelings and needs, especially their fear of food and their inappropriate body images. Bibliography.

Richardson, Diane. *Women and AIDS*. New York: Methuen, 1988.

Comprehensive introductory guide to AIDS and its impact on women.

Richardson outlines symptoms, course of the disease, and modes of transmission while debunking many common myths about AIDS. Individual chapters provide information specifically relevant to lesbians, drug users, sexual partners of people with AIDS, and other women affected by the disease—including women care givers. Concluding chapters recommend policies and consider political implications of AIDS. Source and resource lists, a glossary, and an index.

Rollins, Betty. *First You Cry*. Philadelphia: J. B. Lippincott, 1976. Reprint. New York: New American Library, 1977.
A vivid first-person account by a successful journalist of her experience coping with breast cancer and her subsequent mastectomy. Includes discussion of her self-image, fears, and the impact on her personal life of both the disease and the surgery.

Sandmaier, Marian. *The Invisible Alcoholics: Women and Alcohol Abuse in America*. New York: McGraw-Hill, 1980.
Study of women alcoholics, arguing that society—including professional counselors and researchers—denies their existence and identity while focusing attention on men. Based on interviews with alcoholic women about their experiences, the study concludes that women in male-dominated society often have similar feelings of frustration, pain, and self-destructive tendencies, because they lack access to their own power. Chapters examine the stages and significance of women's alcoholism and include discussion of housewives, employed women, minority women, teenagers, lesbians, and women on Skid Row and in treatment programs. Concludes with women's guide to resources.

Saxton, Marsha, and Florence Howe, eds. *With Wings: An Anthology of Literature by and About Women with Disabilities*. New York: Feminist Press at the City University of New York, 1987.
Collection of stories, poems, and essays by thirty writers with a wide range of disabilities, from blindness to rheumatoid arthritis. Selections address both the pain and the triumphs of living with a disability—and the social barriers disabled people face. The selected writers are activists, students, scholars, and artists—among them nineteenth century writer Mary Wilkins Freeman and poets Adrienne Rich, Muriel Rukeyser, and Alice Walker.

Trien, Susan Flamholtz. *Change of Life: The Menopause Handbook*. New York: Fawcett Columbine, 1986.
A compendium of information about menopause, designed as a guide for older women but offering a good introduction to the issues and problems. A bibliography and notes list other sources. Chapters consider physiological changes, pros and cons of estrogen therapy, nutrition, exercise, sexuality, and os-

teoporosis. "Staying Healthy: A Gynecological Guide" describes a wide range of health issues, including breast cancer. Conclusion includes list of helpful agencies and suggested reading. Tables, figures, illustrations.

Weideger, Paula. *Menstruation and Menopause*. Rev. ed. New York: Dell Books, 1977.
A study of women's experience of menstruation and menopause, based on a survey and research. Weideger describes the physiological processes, sexual and menstrual cycles, cultural taboos surrounding both menstruation and menopause, rites of passage, and the processes' relation to behavior. Discusses medical attitudes and treatments, including home remedies for PMS and menstrual cramps. The purpose of the book is to break women's silence about the experiences of menstruation and menopause, to refute the standard view of both as sicknesses, and to emphasize positive associations. Includes extensive quotations from the survey. Illustrations. Appendix reprints questionnaire from survey. Selected bibliography.

84

FAMILY, HOME, AND RELATIONSHIPS

Marriage and Traditional Families

Arendell, Terry. *Mothers and Divorce: Legal, Economic, and Social Dilemmas.*
Berkeley: University of California Press, 1986.
Discussion of mothers' experience of divorce, based on interviews with sixty
divorced women with children. Arendell opposes the popular view and advice-
book assumptions that divorce is trouble-free and emphasizes the economic
decline suffered by women. She argues that divorce is traumatic for women
because of basic economic inequalities, and she attempts to undermine common stereotypes (that divorce is equally difficult for women and men, that
children inevitably suffer in a divorce, and that women already have equal
rights in divorce). Covers psychological and emotional impact of divorce,
behavior and attitudes of former husbands, and women's experiences with law.
Includes excerpts from interviews. Appendices describe methods and future
research needs. Tables of family and income statistics. Extensive bibliography.

Bernard, Jessie. *The Female World.* New York: Free Press, 1981.
Study of sex-segregated world of women includes lengthy discussions of
women's position in the family, marriage, and kinship networks. Bernard
argues that women spend most of their lives in all-female worlds, even when
married (when social contacts with men become severely restricted). She
describes female-centered family, social, and cultural circles, including the
lives of girls and older women. Bibliography and name and subject indexes.

_____ . *The Future of Marriage.* Cleveland: World Publishing, 1972.
Famous and influential sociological study of marriage in which Bernard proposes the existence of "two marriages," the husband's and the wife's. She
argues that husbands typically enjoy and benefit from marriage far more than
women, who experience higher rates of depression. Bernard predicts that,
while traditional lifelong monogamous marriages will continue to take place,
other forms, including serial monogamy, will predominate in the future. Tables
summarize data on husbands' and wives' relative health and happiness.

Caine, Lynn. *Widow.* New York: William Morrow, 1974.
Personal account of the experience of widowhood by a woman with two
children, widowed after seventeen years of marriage. Caine addresses the
difficulty of coping with grief, adjusting to single identity, and a widow's
position in culture, which Caine describes as "like living in a country where
nobody speaks your language."

Degler, Carl N. *At Odds: Women and the Family in America from the Revolution to the Present*. New York: Oxford University Press, 1980.

Discusses the history of women's role in the American family, emphasizing shifting social structures, changes in family life and in women's status, and the impact of women's work outside the home. Chapters analyze nineteenth century notions of "home," attitudes toward sexuality and reproductive issues, women's contributions to unions, particular stresses on African-American and immigrant families, and the influence of the suffrage movement.

Engels, Friedrich. *The Origin of the Family, Private Property, and the State*. New York: Pathfinder Press, 1972.

Classic and exceptionally influential Marxist analysis (originally published in 1884) of the rise of the nuclear family, from prehistoric times to the nineteenth century. Using early anthropological studies of kinship networks, Engels argues that women's oppression began with the shift from mother-right (women's control over children and property) to father-right and that monogamy developed—with women's consent—to protect women from rape. Although much of Engels' anthropological data are faulty, the book has shaped most later radical discussions of family.

Friedan, Betty. *The Second Stage*. New York: Summit Books, 1981.

Friedan, a prominent feminist and author of *The Feminine Mystique*, argues that the women's movement has moved beyond merely reacting to sexism and must now focus on cooperation with men. The book is controversial in its argument that feminism has ignored family issues, its insistence that sexuality is not political, and the implication that the problems that sparked the movement in the 1960's and 1970's have been solved.

Gutman, Herbert G. *The Black Family in Slavery and Freedom, 1750-1925*. New York: Random House, 1977.

In response to the argument (promoted by Daniel Patrick Moynihan and others) that the black family was "destroyed" by slavery and racism, Gutman argues for the persistence of strong family ties. The bulk of the book is devoted to the period up to 1867, tracing development of slave-kin networks (both families and larger groups), with close attention to meanings of slaves' naming practices and other social patterns. Appendices compare black, Jewish, and Italian households in 1905 New York City and late nineteenth century racial attitudes. Tables, charts, illustrations. Subject and name/title indexes.

Herman, Judith Lewis, with Lisa Hirschman. *Father-Daughter Incest*. Cambridge, Mass.: Harvard University Press, 1981.

Defines and explains father-daughter incest in terms of the dynamics of the traditional, male-dominated family. Herman argues that a father's tremendous power over his children allows him to victimize them sexually and that only major changes in culture—including the improvement of women's status and shifts in the power structure of the family—will abolish incest. Examines family dynamics and the effects of disclosure of incest; proposes remedies, including preventive education. Appendix lists incest laws by state.

Lasch, Christopher. *Haven in a Heartless World: The Family Besieged*. New York: Basic Books, 1977.

History of the American nuclear family, from theories about its origins to the present, including reviews of sociological and other studies. Lasch defines the family as the "last refuge of love and decency" for men but argues that it has been decaying for more than one hundred years because of the socialization of production and reproduction and the obliteration of privacy through the intrusion of the modern world. Explores modern conflicts over privacy, domesticity, marriage, and divorce and claims that the status of the nuclear family as a refuge depends on its isolation from the outside world.

Levitan, Sar A., and Richard S. Belous. *What's Happening to the American Family?* Baltimore: Johns Hopkins University Press, 1981.

Optimistic introductory look at the American family that argues that the family is not disintegrating but changing, with greater plurality and diversity of models. Includes chapters on marriage, family and work, childrearing practices, female-headed households, and government policies. Figures, illustrations.

Owen, Ursula, ed. *Fathers: Reflections by Daughters*. London: Virago, 1983. Reprint. New York: Pantheon Books, 1985.

Personal essays, stories, and poems by women about their fathers, each one introduced by a biographical sketch of the author. The collection includes pieces by novelists Alice Walker, Mary Gordon, and Doris Lessing; work by short-story writer Grace Paley and poet Adrienne Rich; and an essay by Cora Kaplan on poet Elizabeth Barrett Browning and her father. Contributions are interwoven with passages on fathers by historical figures such as Virginia Woolf. Illustrations.

Pogrebin, Letty Cottin. *Family Politics: Love and Power on an Intimate Frontier*. New York: McGraw-Hill, 1983.

An extensive, pro-family feminist examination of the contemporary family and its place in society. Pogrebin draws on current events, social science research, feminist analyses, and mass media to argue that conservative political agendas are actually antifamily and encourage "pedophobia"—hostility toward children. Includes chapters on national family policy, fathering, housework, and pregnancy. Concludes with a call for greater family intimacy based on shared activities.

Russell, Diana E. H. *Rape in Marriage*. New York: Macmillan, 1982.
Groundbreaking examination of marital rape by an activist who helped to establish its criminal status. The study identifies marital rape along a continuum of "normal" sexual behavior in marriage. The data are the first of their kind based on a random sample of women. Sections examine motives and responses of husbands and wives. Includes discussion of the difficulty of persuading legislators and even victims that forced sex within marriage is rape. Appendices summarize selected cases of wife rape and state laws exempting marital rape from prosecution.

Sacks, Karen. "Engels Revisited: Women, the Organization of Production, and Private Property." In *Toward an Anthropology of Women*, edited by Rayna R. Reiter. New York: Monthly Review Press, 1975.
Critique of Engels' influential analysis, using recent cross-cultural studies to claim that women's positions as wives are complexly interrelated to their positions as social adults. Sacks argues that class societies domesticate women's labor, defining it as private work for family use, while men's role is to produce value for social exchange.

Skolnick, Arlene S., and Jerome H. Skolnick, eds. *Family in Transition: Rethinking Marriage, Sexuality, Child Rearing, and Family Organization*. 5th ed. Boston: Little, Brown, 1986.
Collection of essays and book excerpts on a wide range of family issues. Sections address the changing family, gender and sexuality, types of heterosexual couples, relationships between parents and children, and future patterns in family relations. Focus is on a social science view of changing family dynamics, but contributors draw on a broad context and varied perspectives. Brief editors' introductions situate each section and provide short reference lists.

Swerdlow, Amy, Renate Bridenthal, Joan Kelly, and Phyllis Vine. *Household and Kin: Families in Flux*. Old Westbury, N.Y.: Feminist Press, 1981, reprint, 1987.
Survey of the American family, divided into sections covering history, contemporary patterns, and future possibilities. The book uses a broad definition of "family," emphasizing cross-cultural differences and the wide array of alternatives to traditional arrangements. Authors consider rapid recent alterations in the institution of the family, the flexibility of family relations, tensions between tradition and the demands of changing society and economy, and the central role of race, class, and culture in structuring and defining family. Final section includes discussions of Cuba, Israel, Sweden, and alternative families in the United States. Illustrations.

Weitzman, Lenore. *The Divorce Revolution: The Unexpected Social and Economic Consequences for Women and Children in America*. New York: Free Press, 1985.

Study of the economic effects of the no-fault divorce revolution, including considerations about how decisions about marriage and divorce have changed, new conflicts, and the effects of no-fault divorce on marriage, with the major emphasis on the post-divorce status of women and children versus that of men. Weitzman argues that the gender-neutral rules of no-fault divorce conflict with the structural inequalities within marriage, actually impoverishing women and children. (Women experience a 73 percent decline, men a 42 percent rise in their standard of living after divorce.) Chapters address changes in law, property division, alimony awards, custody arrangements, and child support, including the negative impact on children of support provisions that assume men and women can make an equal contribution. Includes quotations from women, statistical data, and discussion of social consequences. Tables, figures. Appendices describe research methods, four hypothetical cases; legal appendix lists state-by-state divorce laws in the United States.

Motherhood

Apple, Rima D. *Mothers and Medicine: A Social History of Infant Feeding, 1890-1950*. Madison: University of Wisconsin Press, 1987.

Apple presents infant feeding as a site where medicine, society, economics, and politics intersect, and where definitions of motherhood, women's role, and the purpose and meaning of science shape what is often considered an instinctive activity. She analyzes the impact of the media, including the use of advertising, emphasizing the role of doctors, scientists, and nonexperts in shaping women's view not only of feeding but also of proper maternal behavior. Chapters address theories and infant-feeding products, related medical practices, the rise of "scientific motherhood," and the periodic shifts back and forth between breast and bottle feeding. Illustrations. Bibliographic essay.

Arditti, Rita, Renate Duelli Klein, and Shelley Minden, eds. *Test-Tube Women: What Future for Motherhood?* Boston: Pandora Press, 1984.

Collection of essays critiquing reproductive technologies. Contributors emphasize the victimization of women and implications of the new technologies for the meaning of motherhood. Essays examine a wide range of technological interventions—from sterilization, contraception, and abortion to embryo transplants—with focus on the potential appropriation of women's reproductive capacities. Glossary, resource list, bibliography.

Bernard, Jessie. *The Future of Motherhood*. New York: Dial Press, 1974.

Influential sociological analysis and critique of motherhood as an American institution. Considers the impact of technology, social and political processes, and changes in the nature of work and in definitions of motherhood. Bernard argues that the Victorian model of "redemptive" motherhood no longer applies and that an integration of women's roles as mother and worker is needed. She predicts a future "new balance" of shared contributions from men and women, with men more involved in "mothering" but not androgynous.

Chesler, Phyllis. *Mothers on Trial: The Battle for Children and Custody*. New York: McGraw-Hill, 1986.
A study of mothers' loss of custody after divorce. Chesler argues that women are tried and punished by loss of custody for being sexually active, lesbians, poor, and otherwise "deviant" from the image of the ideal mother. Chapters address the historical and contemporary situation, notions of parental fitness, specific "crimes" for which women lose custody (including those who are "good enough" mothers but poor or otherwise not ideal), women's position under law, and the international custody situation. Text makes extensive use of quotations and specific individual examples, and notes provide further concrete detail. List of resources for battered women and children, child-support problems, imprisoned mothers, lesbian rights, and others.

——————————. *The Sacred Bond: The Legacy of Baby M*. New York: Times Books, 1988.
Chesler uses the example of the "Baby M" surrogate motherhood trial to examine contemporary attitudes toward motherhood, including the legal and social position of mothers in general. The "sacred bond" of the title is the tie between mother and child, and Chesler argues that Mary Beth Whitehead's fight for custody of "Baby M" is simply an extreme example of the conventional mother's position. Appendices provide relevant court documents, including the original surrogacy agreement between Whitehead and William Stern.

Chodorow, Nancy. *The Reproduction of Mothering: Psychoanalysis and the Sociology of Gender*. Berkeley: University of California Press, 1978.
A major and influential feminist rewriting of Freudian psychology of women, focusing on the "reproduction"—that is, the learning—of mothering behavior. Much of the argument examines the impact of the mother-daughter relationship on the later development of bonding between women and female nurturance. In contrast to the Freudian theory that girls shift allegiance from mother to father, Chodorow argues that a girl's identification with and love of her mother is a crucial shaping influence on her development.

Dally, Ann. *Inventing Motherhood: The Consequences of an Ideal*. New York: Schocken Books, 1983.
Examination of contemporary "crisis of motherhood"—the increasing isola-

tion of mothers and women's profound anxiety over whether to have children. Chapters discuss the modern idealization of maternity, First and Second Wave feminism's attitudes toward motherhood, changes in child-care doctrine and social policy, and men as fathers. Concludes with a call for increased social status for parenting, male participation, and advance planning within families.

Downrick, Stephanie, and Sibyl Grundberg, eds. *Why Children?* New York: Harcourt Brace Jovanovich, 1980.
Eighteen personal essays by women with and without children. Contributors include married and single women, lesbians and heterosexuals. Essays examine choices about childbearing, social and family pressure, and the influence of feminism on these women's decisions. Illustrations.

Fabe, Marilyn, and Norma Wikler. *Up Against the Clock: Career Women Speak on the Choice to Have Children.* New York: Random House, 1979.
Interviews with ten women about how they decided whether to have children. The study emphasizes choice, and "Examining the Issues" sections draw on additional interviews for ideas about social pressures and implications. Includes discussions of single mothering, adoption, and choosing to remain childless.

Friday, Nancy. *My Mother/Myself: The Daughter's Search for Identity.* New York: Dell Books, 1978.
Popular examination of mother-daughter relationships, defining them as central to the daughters' development. Argues that the "symbiotic" relationship between mother and daughter creates tension and can make it difficult for the daughter to break the bond and move from dependence to a separate adult identity. Also emphasizes the impact of the mother's attitudes and self-image on the daughter.

Friedland, Ronnie, and Carol Kort, eds. *The Mothers' Book: Shared Experiences.* Boston: Houghton Mifflin, 1981.
Essays and poems by women about their experiences as mothers. Includes descriptions of and reactions to pregnancy, childbirth, and postpartum experiences; sexuality; work; self-image; relationships with family and friends; and difficulties of dealing with miscarriage, stillbirth, and disabled children. Although most perspectives are positive, all acknowledge ambivalence, tensions, and the process of learning how to mother. Illustrations.

Genevie, Louis, and Eva Margolies. *The Motherhood Report: How Women Feel about Being Mothers.* New York: Macmillan, 1987.
Results of a 1985 survey of eleven hundred American mothers between the ages

of eighteen and eighty. Sections discuss their reasons for having children; the changing stresses of motherhood; joy, anger, and other emotions; stages from pregnancy through mothering adult children; relationships between mothers and children; mothering children with disabilities; adoption; and work and family, including chapters on fathers and on single mothers. Conclusion argues that ambivalence is the norm in mothers' attitudes but that 96 percent would do it again. Appendix explains research methods and provides questionnaire.

Gerson, Kathleen. *Hard Choices: How Women Decide About Work, Career, and Motherhood*. Berkeley: University of California Press, 1985.
Interviews with women reaching adulthood in the 1970's examine their work aspirations and attitudes toward motherhood and home. Argues that women's choices are influenced by widespread structural changes in marital arrangements, the workplace, and the economy. Includes excerpts from interviews and figures summarizing data. Appendices provide tables, methodology of survey, sample characteristics, and the interview questionnaire itself. Bibliography.

Gordon, Linda. "Voluntary Motherhood: The Beginnings of the Birth-Control Movement." In her *Woman's Body, Woman's Right*. New York: Viking Press, 1976.
Gordon examines the early movement (from the 1870's onward) for reproductive freedom and related notions of motherhood. She argues that birth-control activists, many of them feminists or moral reformers, contrasted "voluntary" with "involuntary" motherhood, advocating sexual abstinence or contraception as the best way to enable women to devote themselves to childrearing because they would be freed from constant childbearing.

Greif, Geoffrey M., and Mary S. Pabst. *Mothers Without Custody*. Lexington, Mass.: Lexington Books/D. C. Heath, 1988.
Examination of non-custodial mothers, emphasizing recent changes in custody arrangements, and the variety of reasons that women are denied or choose not to seek custody of their children. Explores contemporary attitudes, particularly the common assumption that a woman who chooses to give up custody is abnormal; how custody decisions are made; and subsequent relationships between mother and children. Includes in-depth discussion of several women's experiences and an interview with a family in which the father has custody. Appendix provides statistical tables. Lengthy bibliography.

Klein, Carol. *Mothers and Sons*. Boston: G. K. Hall, 1985.
A discussion of the bonds between mothers and sons from pregnancy and birth through adulthood. Klein considers questions of power, both in the family and in society; sexuality, including homosexuality; sex roles, feminism, and various types of conflict between mothers and sons. Includes many personal accounts

based on questionnaires and interviews of five hundred women and two hundred men. The responses address mothers' central role in their sons' lives and development; the tensions between providing security and letting go of sons in later life; sons' responses to mothers in childhood and as adults; the impact of the mother-son relationship on men's attitudes toward other women, their self-esteem, and other issues.

Lazarre, Jane. *The Mother Knot.* New York: McGraw-Hill, 1976.
Personal account of a woman's experience of the first three years of motherhood. Lazarre describes her emotional and physical state, the pressures and changes she experienced—including her changing sense of self and the development of her identity as a mother; and, since she is a partner in an interracial marriage, the impact of racism on her experience of mothering.

Leavitt, Judith Walzer. *Brought to Bed: Childbearing in America, 1750-1950.* New York: Oxford University Press, 1986.
Detailed history of childbearing drawing extensively on personal accounts by women. The study's emphasis on the crucial role of networks of female friends and relatives posits the entry into motherhood as a women-centered rite of passage but one whose meaning changed when childbirth moved from a home-based experience dominated by women to a hospital-based medical procedure controlled by male physicians. Includes chronology of childbirth history, glossary of medical terms. Illustrations.

Luker, Kristin. "Motherhood and Morality in America." In her *Abortion and the Politics of Motherhood.* Berkeley: University of California Press, 1984.
Analyzes the current abortion debate as "a referendum on the place and meaning of motherhood," situating views of pro-choice and antiabortion activists in the context of cultural attitudes toward motherhood. Luker argues that the two sides define motherhood differently, with antiabortionists placing biological (women's reproductive role) before social (women as paid workers) facts of life.

McKaughan, Molly. *The Biological Clock: Reconciling Careers and Motherhood in the 1980s.* New York: Doubleday, 1987.
Based on a survey of "clock watchers"—American women who postponed the decision about whether to have children. Examines reasons for postponing childbearing, attitudes toward work and possible tensions between career and family, effects on marriage, physical and emotional implications of postponement, and experiences of single and older women. Personal responses and anecdotes from interview subjects and author are integrated into narrative. Bibliography.

Margolis, Maxine L. *Mothers and Such: Views of American Women and Why They Changed.* Berkeley: University of California Press, 1984.

Margolis, an anthropologist, analyzes changing views of women and mother-hood through the principle of cultural materialism (the idea that changes in the material base of experience gradually lead to changes in social and political structures). The focus is on middle-class American women, and chapters trace the history of attitudes toward motherhood and mothers, home and homemaking, notions of "woman's place," and women's changing roles. The concluding chapter, "She Has Only Herself to Blame," identifies victim-blaming as a "system-maintaining ideology" used not only about rape and other forms of assault against women but also to "explain" women's economic and work status and other aspects of women's secondary position in society. Epilogue argues that changes in the material conditions of women's lives, rather than the feminist movement, have led to recent changes in women's consciousness and guarantee that there can be no real return to "traditional" values. Illustrations.

O'Brien, Mary. *The Politics of Reproduction.* Boston: Routledge & Kegan Paul, 1981.

Theoretical analysis of men's and women's "reproductive consciousness," arguing that people's attitudes toward the world are shaped by their gender-based relationship to reproduction. Thus, men feel alienated from the lifecycle because they cannot guarantee that children are their own, women connected to it because they give birth and therefore experience the connection directly. O'Brien's argument is controversial in its combination of Marxist and radical feminist theory but influential in its attempt to explore possible connections between reproductive roles and worldviews.

Pogrebin, Letty Cottin. "The Politics of Pregnancy and Motherhood." In her *Family Politics: Love and Power on an Intimate Frontier.* New York: McGraw-Hill, 1983.

Examines the abortion controversy on the basis of the idea that women as a group are socially and culturally defined by motherhood. Pogrebin considers double standards (racism, economic privilege) that limit choice and argues that the central question in family politics is "Who's in charge of motherhood?"

Rich, Adrienne. *Of Woman Born: Motherhood as Experience and Institution.* New York: W. W. Norton, 1976.

A classic feminist examination of motherhood looks at both personal experiences and how mothering is institutionalized. Rich, a prominent American poet, argues that the experience of mothering is shaped by negative cultural assumptions about women's roles. Incorporates anecdotes about Rich's own experience as the mother of sons, including reflections on mothering in the 1950's.

Ryder, Norman B. "The Future of American Fertility." In *Women and Work: Problems and Perspectives*, edited by Rachel Kahn-Hut, Arlene Kaplan Daniels, and Richard Colvard. New York: Oxford University Press, 1982.

Discusses the American trend toward lower fertility, arguing that women's increasing access to the workplace has made full-time mothering less appealing. Proposes that government not implement policies to reverse the trend, and that coming demographic changes need not be disastrous.

Weiner, Lynn Y. *From Working Girl to Working Mother: The Female Labor Force in the United States, 1820-1980*. Chapel Hill: University of North Carolina Press, 1985.

This study of changes in women's participation in the work force considers the role of changing ideas about motherhood in the movement from single, self-supporting women workers to a female labor force dominated by married women and mothers. Weiner traces debates over the relationship between motherhood and women's work, particularly the shift from the nineteenth century emphasis on "future motherhood" (with all women defined as mothers-to-be) to the contemporary acknowledgment of women's economic need for paid work. She also considers historical and more recent controversies over the effects of women's work on their ability to mother, and policy issues such as day care. Tables, figures. Lengthy bibliography, including manuscript sources.

Sex Roles, Gender Stereotypes, and Childrearing

Astrachan, Anthony. *How Men Feel: Their Responses to Women's Demands for Equality and Power*. Garden City, N.Y.: Anchor Press/Doubleday, 1986.

Discussion of men's reactions to feminism, anchored in the author's personal attempt to understand changing expectations and based on interviews with other men. Sections cover work, family life, and sexuality, with chapters on the "men's movement" (feminist and antifeminist men's organizations) and changing male roles. Though Astrachan is sympathetic to feminism, in his conclusion he claims that most men have a negative response to recent changes in the social and cultural status of women.

Basow, Susan A. *Gender Stereotypes: Traditions and Alternatives*. 2d ed. Monterey, Calif.: Brooks/Cole, 1986.

Introductory review and critique of gender stereotypes, covering physical, cognitive, social, personal, behavioral, and sexual roles. Includes discussion of origins, theories, and consequences of sex roles and stereotypes, with an eye to moving beyond them. Considers socialization through television and other media, the impact of gender stereotypes on romantic and other relationships, and the effects of stereotypes on power relations, work, and legal status. Figures, tables, illustrations. Lengthy reference list, name and subject indexes.

Belotti, Elena Gianini. *What Are Little Girls Made Of? The Roots of Feminine Stereotypes*. Introduction by Margaret Mead. New York: Schocken Books, 1976.
Examination of sex-role stereotypes and their manifestations from birth to elementary school. Argues that despite social changes, limiting stereotypes still exist and are influential even before birth. Stereotypes are promoted by media, schools, home, toys, and books. Women's treatment of female children is in turn influenced by stereotyped attitudes (for example, female babies are seen as more troublesome than male babies). Examines the traditional roots of attitudes (including those toward male sexuality), women as servers of men and children, and differences in approaches to play.

Brooks-Gunn, Jeanne, and Wendy Schempp Matthews. *He and She: How Children Develop Their Sex-Role Identity*. Englewood Cliffs, N.J.: Prentice-Hall, 1979.
Combines anecdotal and empirical information to examine the development of sex roles, from prenatal influences through adolescence. Begins with the social context for sex-role stereotypes and biological foundations for sex differences (genetic influences, physiological differences, studies on effects of hormone exposure). Compares stereotypes with studies on parental behavior to examine possible sources of "masculine" and "feminine" identities, arguing that "mediators of sex-typed behavior" are everywhere (parents, teachers, television). Tables, figures, illustrations.

Filene, Peter Gabriel. *Him/Her/Self: Sex Roles in Modern America*. New York: Harcourt Brace Jovanovich, 1975. Reprint. New York: New American Library, 1976.
History of development of contemporary sex roles in the United States, discussed in sections addressing the end of the Victorian era (1890-1919) and more recent decades (1920-1974). Filene traces various aspects of sex roles, from debates about women's enfranchisement and public role to transgressions of traditional etiquette (such as smoking in public), with chapters on "men and manliness" and on "the long amnesia" (the Depression, World War II, and the 1950's—during which time little seemed to change). Concludes with chapter on recent changes in roles, including the impact of the political movements of the 1970's. Appendix provides statistics on female labor force from 1890 to 1970. Bibliographic essay.

Giele, Janet Zollinger. *Women and the Future: Changing Sex Roles in Modern America*. New York: Free Press, 1978.
Reviews research examining sex roles in the light of the changes brought about by the women's movement. Issues include the impact on work, relations be-

tween men and women, family and family policy, and women's education Giele argues that such changes affect men and women equally and that they have the potential to alter all established institutions. Tables, figures.

Gilder, George. *Sexual Suicide*. New York: Quadrangle, 1974.
Controversial antifeminist book arguing for the innateness and central importance of sex differences. Gilder claims that feminism threatens "procreative sexuality," leading to the disintegration of nuclear family (which depends on men's subordination of violent sexuality to women's "futurity") and the destruction of work as a symbol of masculinity. Argues that women's role as mothers is "the central activity of the human community," and what feminists call sexism is actually the "exaltation" of women. Bibliography.

Kimball, Gayle. *50-50 Parenting: Sharing Family Rewards and Responsibilities*. Lexington, Mass.: Lexington Books/ D. C. Heath, 1988.
Study of shared parenting based on interviews with children, parents, family experts, and "progressive" employers. Considers the impact of co-parenting on children, working women, marriage, and relationships between children and fathers. Book begins with a self-test and children's report to analyze degree of co-parenting and ends with surveys for parents, children. Chapters examine the advantages of equal parenting; co-parenting in marriage, after divorce, and after remarriage; step-parenting; communal parenting; employers' policies; and unequal parenting as frequent strain on marriage. Conclusion considers the future of parenting and the impact of feminism and men's rights groups on notions of equal parenting, and speculates about the potential influence of reproductive technologies. Kimball argues that multiple roles—including men's involvement in fathering—produce greater happiness and fulfillment. Appendices describe details of study, children in sample, other research, and resource guide.

Leone, Bruno, and M. Teresa O'Neill, eds. *Male/Female Roles: Opposing Viewpoints*. St. Paul, Minn.: Greenhaven Press, 1983.
Collection of essays debating issues surrounding sex roles. Sections cover how sex roles are established, whether women are oppressed, whether men need liberating, and the future of the family. Includes reprints from prominent voices in the debate, among them Betty Friedan, Phyllis Schlafly, George Gilder, and Ellen Goodman. The book is part of an "opposing viewpoints" series. Each essay begins with questions to consider while reading, and sections conclude with suggestions on how to sort out fact from opinion. Bibliography, index.

Pogrebin, Letty Cottin. *Growing Up Free: Raising Your Child in the 80s*. New York: McGraw-Hill, 1980. Reprint. New York: Bantam Books, 1981.

A guide to nonsexist childrearing, including reviews of research in the area. Pogrebin offers explanations of the disadvantages of sex-role stereotyping, from pre-birth biases onward. The book takes an introductory approach but provides extensive footnotes to scholarly sources.

Spock, Benjamin. *Dr. Spock on Parenting*. New York: Simon & Schuster, 1988.
Chatty and accessible advice from the most influential parenting expert of the 1950's and 1960's. Includes discussion of working mothers and day care, and the long chapter "Being a Father Today," with a section on "teaching sexual equality." Also included are personal reminiscences about Spock's own experience as a father, doctor, and stepfather. Much of the book originally appeared in *Redbook*, and Spock makes use of questions from parents and readers to organize advice.

Stockard, Jean, and Miriam M. Johnson. *Sex Roles: Sex Inequality and Sex Role Development*. Englewood Cliffs, N.J.: Prentice-Hall, 1980.
Sociological introduction to sex roles in the context of male-dominated society. Emphasizes the American experience, discussing economic and political aspects, sex roles in the family, biological and psychological differences between the sexes, education, psychoanalytic explanations, and roles across the life cycle. Concludes with a chapter on a "future without male dominance," in which men would become more like women—for instance, nurturance would be valued over aggression and cultural symbols would reflect equal valuation of men and women. Lengthy reference list, with short suggested readings after each chapter.

Tavris, Carol, and Carole Wade. "Getting the Message: The Learning Perspective." In their *The Longest War: Sex Differences in Perspective*. New York: Harcourt Brace Jovanovich, 1977. Reprint. 1984.
Introductory discussion of sex-role socialization from feminist perspective. Focuses on sources of gender patterns (parents, media, teachers) and consequences (especially female lack of self-esteem and male interest in achievement). Includes a self-analyzing androgyny index based on standard clinical scale.

Tiger, Lionel. *Men in Groups*. New York: Random House, 1969. 2d ed., with new preface. New York: Marion Boyars, 1984.
Conservative sociobiological analysis of male bonding, defined as the essential evolutionary element of human nature and epitomized in prehistoric male hunting pack. Tiger argues that men are inherently aggressive and that modern bonding is visible in arenas such as war and competition. Critics say the extrapolation of human behavior from animal studies overlooks profound differences. Bibliography.

Weitz, Shirley. *Sex Roles: Biological, Psychological, and Social Foundations*. New York: Oxford University Press, 1977.

Social psychology analysis of biological (including aggression, sexuality), psychological (socialization), and social (family, symbolism) "maintenance systems" for traditional sex roles. Argues that it is necessary to understand foundations in order to change roles. Weitz claims male and female roles operate in tandem and thus cannot be understood or changed separately. The conclusion, which describes changes in sex roles, includes analysis and critique of the situation in the Soviet Union, Sweden, China, and Israel. Includes discussion of the impact of the past and present American women's movements. Each section contains suggested readings.

Nontraditional Families

Bohannon, Paul. *All the Happy Families: Exploring the Varieties of Family Life*. New York: McGraw-Hill, 1985.

Survey of the contemporary American family focusing on divorce, single-parent families, and step-families. Bohannon argues that families have been "abandoned by society" and that specific forms of family life are less important than encouraging social commitment to family through a social agenda that acknowledges realities (such as women working outside home). Advocates "well-family industry," instead of what he describes as the current "divorce industry." Bibliographic essay.

Bozett, Frederick W., ed. *Gay and Lesbian Parents*. New York: Praeger, 1987.

Essays about gay and lesbian parents, including sections on the parents themselves, their children, alternative families, and psychosocial and legal implications of gay and lesbian parenting. The book is aimed at professionals (therapists, social workers, family-policy experts), but the collection is extremely useful for other readers because it includes literature reviews, summaries of other research, and discussions of policy implications. Among contributions directly addressing the experience of women are Barbara M. McCandlish's "Against all Odds: Lesbian Mother Family Dynamics," G. Dorsey Green's "Lesbian Mothers: Mental Health Considerations," and Alisa Steckel's "Psychosocial Development of Children of Lesbian Mothers."

Fabe, Marilyn, and Norma Wikler. "Going It Alone as a Single Mother." In their *Up Against the Clock: Career Women Speak on the Choice to Have Children*. New York: Random House, 1979.

Interviews with three women—one a lesbian—who chose to have a child on their own. Deals with financial issues, social pressures, childbirth, day care, and conflicts between work and mothering.

Friedland, Ronnie, and Carol Kort, eds. "Becoming a Single Mother," "Becoming a Stepmother," and "Foster, Adoptive, and Natural Mothers." In their *The Mother's Book: Shared Experiences*. Boston: Houghton Mifflin, 1981.
Personal accounts by women about their experiences as mothers in nontraditional families. Short essays consider tensions and triumphs and focus on specific points in individual women's lives.

Genevie, Louis, and Eva Margolies. "Single Motherhood." In their *The Motherhood Report: How Women Feel About Being Mothers*. New York: Macmillan, 1987.
Part of a large survey on mothering. The responses suggest that single mothers in general manage to cope on their own, although they often feel overwhelmed by having sole responsibility for children (and some think that their children urgently need a father). But benefits include more time to spend with their child, a closer relationship, and less conflict because there is no other parent with whom to confer.

McKaughan, Molly. "The Single-Mother Option" and "Single Mothers: And Baby Makes Two." In her *The Biological Clock: Reconciling Careers and Motherhood in the 1980s*. New York: Doubleday, 1987.
Within a survey of women who postponed motherhood, these chapters use personal accounts by survey subjects to examine how women make the decision to become single parents and how they cope with parenting alone. Includes discussion of how women choose fathers (from friends to artificial insemination), economic considerations, and fathers' rights.

Maglin, Nan Bauer, and Nancy Schniedwind, eds. *Women and Stepfamilies: Voices of Anger and Love*. Philadelphia: Temple University Press, 1989.
A collection of personal essays and interviews about women's experiences of step-families. Contributors address both the conflicts and the satisfactions of their family lives and include women who are mothers, stepmothers, stepdaughters, and stepgrandmothers, lesbian and heterosexual partners, and participants in married and unmarried families. Essays are written from a variety of perspectives based on racial and ethnic identity, class, and employment. Editors' introduction. Bibliography, index.

Pies, Cheri. *Considering Parenthood: A Workbook for Lesbians*. San Francisco: Spinster/Aunt Lute, 1985.
Although meant as a guide for lesbians thinking about becoming parents, this book provides a comprehensive consideration of lesbian parenting and issues confronting alternative families in general. Explores emotional and practical issues (from financial concerns to various means of conception), stressing the importance of a support network. Includes discussions of possible living and family arrangements (co-parenting, single parenting, and so on), parenting for

disabled lesbians, and relationships with men. "Exercises" throughout the
book are designed to help readers make decisions. Appendices list useful
support and resource groups and consider health issues, including AIDS.
Bibliography.

Wolf, Deborah Goleman. "Lesbian Mothers." In her *The Lesbian Community*.
Berkeley: University of California Press, 1979, 2d ed., with preface and afterword, 1980.
Overview of lesbian mothering. Includes discussion of legal problems concerning custody, development of self-help groups in the early 1970's, and relationships between lesbian mothers and their children (including issues about children's sexuality). Though part of a larger study of the San Francisco lesbian
community, this chapter deals with broad issues and national groups.

Domesticity and Housework

Andre, Rae. *Homemakers: The Forgotten Workers*. Chicago: University of Chicago
Press, 1981.
Study of homemakers with emphasis on the movement to change their status.
Andre underlines connections between homemaking and other social roles and
definitions of work and personal life; she criticizes sex-role stereotyping and
the devaluation of homemaking. Includes interviews and some cross-cultural
comparisons. Appendices provide "National Platforms for Homemakers'
Rights" and additional sources. Bibliography.

Beer, William R. *Househusbands: Men and Housework in American Families*. New
York: Praeger, 1983.
Sociological study of men's attitudes toward housework, based on a survey of
fifty-six white American "househusbands"—men who have partially or to-
tally taken over the responsibility for housework. Beer begins by reviewing
recent changes in sex roles and other studies on work and on women and
housework and concludes that men feel much as women do about housework—both frustrated with it and satisfied by it. Text opens with a description
of the author's own experience sharing domestic work and child care and
includes many quotes from the survey.

Burstyn, Joan N. *Victorian Education and the Ideal of Womanhood*. New York:
Barnes & Noble Books, 1980. Reprint. New Brunswick, N.J.: Rutgers University Press, 1984.
Analysis of the prevailing Victorian notion of "separate spheres"—the identification of men with the public sphere of work, politics, and finance, women
with the private world of home, family, and domesticity. Burstyn argues that

the battle over women's access to higher education was a major site of conflict but that the struggle was actually about the culture's ideal vision of womanhood and women's confinement to private concerns. Illustrations. Select bibliography.

Cowan, Ruth Schwartz. *More Work for Mother: The Ironies of Household Technology from the Open Hearth to the Microwave*. New York: Basic Books, 1983.
Cowan's study argues that new inventions and technological advances actually lead women to spend more time on housework than they did two hundred years ago. Discusses escalating standards that feed into consumer economy, such as the insistence on spotless homes made possible by "labor-saving" devices; the cultural refusal to take seriously alternative solutions (such as communal living); and the underlying assumption that housework is done by full-time homemakers.

Matthews, Glenna. *"Just a Housewife": The Rise and Fall of Domesticity in America*. New York: Oxford University Press, 1987.
Traces changes in attitudes toward domesticity from the eighteenth century, when home was the center of life and homemaking was highly valued, through the nineteenth century relegation of women to the "separate sphere" of home, to the twentieth century denigration of housewives' work. Matthews looks at fictional portrayals, personal experiences of prominent American women, the influence of Charles Darwin, and technological advances. Argues that the development of consumer culture is partly responsible for the devaluation of housework.

Minton, Michael H., with Jean Libman Block. *What Is a Wife Worth?* New York: William Morrow, 1983. Reprint. New York: McGraw-Hill, 1984.
Economic analysis of the value of a homemaker as demonstrated by legal awards in divorce settlements. Minton's goal is to give women who work in the home a sense of worth, but his context is divorce and the economic situation of the displaced homemaker. Includes brief history of marriage and women's legal status, recent changes in marital property and divorce laws. Economic value is figured on the basis of the salary required to provide equivalent services, plus "opportunities forgone" by homemakers. Appendix provides chart for figuring monetary value.

Oakley, Ann. *Woman's Work: The Housewife, Past and Present*. New York: Vintage Books, 1976.
Traces the development of the role of housewife from preindustrial society to the present. Argues that the unpaid and menial nature of housework and its close association with traditional notions of femininity contribute to women's low status. Oakley claims that industrialization has worsened the situation by

removing men from the site of women's domestic work and that women's
entry into the paid work force merely doubles their work responsibilities.
Includes interviews with four housewives and cross-cultural studies. Based on
British examples, but the conclusions are applicable to the United States.
Source list.

Palmer, Phyllis. "Housework and Domestic Labor: Racial and Technological
Change." In *My Troubles Are Going to Have Trouble with Me: Everyday Trials
and Triumphs of Women Workers*, edited by Karen Brodkin Sacks and Dorothy
Remy. New Brunswick, N.J.: Rutgers University Press, 1984.
Analysis of changes in black women's role as domestic workers as such work
shifts from "private" (servants in homes) to "public" (service sector). Author
argues that race is used to obscure changes in definitions of service work.
Essay contrasts the reality of such labor with both black women's hopes that
domestic work would be seen as a "craft" and middle-class white women's
recent view of homemaking as "management."

Strasser, Susan. *Never Done: A History of American Housework*. New York: Pantheon Books, 1982.
A descriptive history of housework, personalized by the use of excerpts from
autobiographical writings and vivid portraits of housekeeping activities.
Strasser traces technological and cultural changes in cleaning and food-
preparation through contemporary fast-food restaurants and presents the history of housework as a reflection of fundamental changes in American daily
life. Includes dozens of photographs and illustrations of implements, advertisements, and women performing household tasks. Bibliographic essay.

Family-Related Policy Issues

Baxandall, Rosalyn F. "Who Shall Care for Our Children? The History and Development of Day Care in the United States." In *Women: A Feminist Perspective*, edited by Jo Freeman. Palo Alto, Calif.: Mayfield, 1975.
History of day care in the United States, from the 1830's founding of the
country's first infant school. The essay examines the need for day care, with
statistics on working mothers, and the impact of attitudes toward women's
work and psychiatric and social workers' ideas about the mother-child relationship. Argues that day care is a "universal entitlement," like public education, and that it should be financed by federal government. According to
Baxandall, the absence of federally funded day care functions as a work dis-
incentive, because private solutions are too expensive for most working women.

Giele, Janet Zollinger. "Family Policy." In her *Women and the Future: Changing
Sex Roles in Modern America*. New York: Free Press, 1978.

Reviews studies on and policies toward social programs, government policies, and informal community structures in the light of the growing sex-symmetry in family life. Discussion covers child care, welfare, Social Security, community service, and support networks.

Hewlett, Sylvia Ann. *A Lesser Life: The Myth of Women's Liberation in America.* New York: William Morrow, 1986.
Controversial examination of modern feminism's impact on women. Hewlett argues that the battle for the ERA and other equal-rights-oriented legislation actually heightened women's economic vulnerability, increasing conflicts between work and family and stripping women of protection in case of divorce. "A Personal View" describes Hewlett's own problems integrating work and motherhood. Illustrations, anecdotal case histories.

Kirp, David L., Mark G. Yudof, and Marlene Strong Franks. "Gender Policy and the Forms of Family." In their *Gender Justice*. Chicago: University of Chicago Press, 1986.
Analysis of the need for a family policy "attentive to present circumstances"—that is, sensitive to a broad range of choices and providing support for nurturing children and other dependents. Reviews and critiques policies on divorce-related issues (domicile, support, marriage contracts, alimony, custody) and those policies related to stable families, particularly income tax and child care policies. The authors advocate family allowance (versus government-run day-care centers). Chapter explores the tensions between preserving the privacy of family life and the necessity of policies because of the public impact of the family, arguing that government intervention should be limited and unobtrusive.

Lefkowitz, Rochelle, and Ann Withorn, eds. *For Crying Out Loud: Women and Poverty in the United States*. New York: Pilgrim Press, 1986.
Collection of essays and personal accounts of women's experience of poverty. Includes critiques of American welfare system and strategies for change in social policies. Among the contributions is "Reports from the Front: Welfare Mothers up in Arms," an essay by members of a welfare-rights group that describes the Catch-22's of the AFDC system, arguing that bureaucratic policies deny families control over their lives.

Levitan, Sar A., and Richard S. Belous. "Family Policies: Shoring Up the Haven?" In their *What's Happening to the American Family?* Baltimore, Md.: Johns Hopkins University Press, 1981.
Compares U.S. policies with Swedish and West German policies and analyzes U.S. government support services. The authors argue that government family

policies must pay attention to changes in family life and structures, rather than reinforcing the traditional nuclear family. Figures, illustrations.

Lipman-Blumen, Jean, and Jessie Bernard, eds. *Sex Roles and Social Policy: A Complex Social Science Equation*. Sage Studies in International Sociology 14. Beverly Hills, Calif.: Sage Publications, 1979.
A collection of essays from an international perspective, exploring the possible impact of social science research on public policy on sex roles. Essays consider connections between research and policy, European and Asian examples of deliberate family policy, women as policymakers and agents of change, and the future outlook. Editors' concluding essay emphasizes the necessity of cross-cultural coalitions among women researchers, activists, and policymakers. Subject and author indexes.

McKaughan, Molly. "The Child Care Conundrum." In her *The Biological Clock: Reconciling Careers and Motherhood in the 1980s*. New York: Doubleday, 1987.
Part of a survey of women who have postponed childbearing. This chapter discusses possible solutions to child-care problems, emphasizing the distance between ideals proposed by experts and "real choices" (although focus is on middle-class women with access to paid caretakers). Uses personal accounts by survey subjects to discuss pros and cons of various solutions (from live-in help to day-care centers) and mothers' coping strategies.

Pogrebin, Letty Cottin. "Home Economics: National Policy vs. The Family Interest." In her *Family Politics: Love and Power on an Intimate Frontier*. New York: McGraw-Hill, 1983.
Outlines national policies that Pogrebin believes would support real family life rather than the ideal of the patriarchal family. Includes proposals for housing and employment programs, tax reform, family subsidies, and wider provision of social services.

Rodgers, Harrell R., Jr. "Reforming the American Welfare System." In his *Poor Women, Poor Families: The Economic Plight of America's Female Headed Families*. Armonk, N.Y.: M. E. Sharpe, 1986.
Rodgers proposes wide-ranging reforms of government policies on families and welfare. Calls for government commitment to sex education and family planning, some version of a family allowance, child care, enforcement of child-support awards, emphasis on quality education for the poor, development of good job programs, and passage of comparable worth legislation. Advocates an increase in housing assistance and nutrition programs.

Sidel, Ruth. "A Call for a U.S. Family Policy." In her *Women and Children Last: The Plight of Poor Women in Affluent America*. New York: Viking Press, 1986.

This study of women and poverty analyzes flaws in the current welfare system. Sidel proposes revamping of the entire system and the institution of a new national family policy guaranteeing women's equal access to employment, prenatal and other health care, universal maternity and child-care leave, affordable day care, and enforcement of child-support awards.

Steiner, Gilbert Y. *The Futility of Family Policy*. Washington, D.C.: Brookings Institution, 1981.
Analysis of the development of family policy as a political issue, with focus on evolution of "the family problem" and its definition by liberals and conservatives. Steiner insists on the impossibility of creating overarching political solutions to what are essentially questions of values and the impossibility of reconciling conflicting expectations of behavior and family structure. Includes chapters on child abuse and neglect, and comparison with European models.

Watkins, Kathleen Pullan, and Lucius Durant, Jr. *Day Care: A Source Book*. New York: Garland, 1988.
A broad overview of the day-care field through introductory essays and annotated bibliographies, including considerations of administration and management of day-care centers; roles and responsibilities of teachers and "care givers"; various types of programs and their components; working with parents; evaluating programs; and future directions and issues, including criticism by day-care opponents. The types of centers discussed include those for infants and toddlers, family and home-based centers, and those for school-aged children. Although aimed at day-care providers, the information is a useful guide to the issues and including resources.

Zigler, Edward F., and Meryl Frank, eds. *The Parental Leave Crisis: Toward a National Policy*. New Haven, Conn.: Yale University Press, 1988.
Essays examining a range of issues surrounding the development of parental leave policies. Contributors review the histories of the family and of maternal leave, consider varieties of infant- and child-care strategies, and survey policies in the United States and elsewhere. Several essays discuss economic, legal, and other implications of state-implemented policies. U.S. Representative Patricia Schroeder argues for a federal parental-leave policy that recognizes contemporary economic realities. The staff of the Yale Bush Center Advisory Committee on Infant Care Leave recommends a new federal policy, including income replacement, benefit continuation, and job protection. Tables. Index.

Zimmerman, Shirley L. *Understanding Family Policy: Theoretical Approaches*. Newbury Park, Calif.: Sage Publications, 1988.
Study of family policy theory: how to understand and analyze family policies, with applications for policy frameworks. Emphasizes policy's function as a

response to family stress, with arguments illustrated by chapters on specific policies for families of the mentally retarded and the elderly disabled. Zimmerman concludes that social policy fills needs that the market cannot or will not meet. She argues for the application of a family framework to policy discussion, urging attention to the impact of policy on families, rather than the recent focus on issues of traditional versus nontraditional families. Study employs a broad definition of "family." Appendix summarizes major concepts. Tables and figures.

PSYCHOLOGY

Traditional Psychological Theories on Women

Deutsch, Helene. *The Psychology of Women: A Psychoanalytic Interpretation.*
2 vols. New York: Bantam Books, 1973.
One of the standard psychoanalytic studies of female psychology, emphasizing
"normal" women (unlike much of Freud's work, which emphasizes psycho-
pathology). Volume 1, *Girlhood*, traces psychological development, including
what Deutsch calls the "three essential traits of femininity": narcissism, pas-
sivity, and masochism. Volume 2, *Motherhood*, describes women's "role as
servant of the species."

Freud, Sigmund. "Some Psychical Consequences of the Anatomical Distinction
Between the Sexes" (1925), "Female Sexuality" (1931), and "Femininity"
(1933). In *The Standard Edition of the Complete Psychological Works of Sigmund Freud*, edited by James Strachey. 24 vols. London: Hogarth Press,
1953-1974.
Freud's most important—and most controversial—essays on the psychology
of women and female sexuality. Taken together, they describe and explain his
theories of penis envy, the castration and Oedipus complexes, and girls' re-
direction of desire from father to mother.

Grosskurth, Phyllis. *Melanie Klein: Her World and Her Work.* New York: Alfred A.
Knopf, 1980.
Life of an important woman psychoanalyst (1882-1960) famous for her work
with disturbed children and theories on child development. Includes discussions of Klein's conflicts with Freud and his daughter Anna (also known for
her contributions to psychoanalytic child-development theory). Illustrations.
Chronology and bibliography of Klein's works.

Maccoby, Eleanor Emmons, and Carol Nagy Jacklin. *The Psychology of Sex Differences.* Stanford, Calif.: Stanford University Press, 1974.
Analysis of intellectual, behavioral, and social differences and similarities
between women and men, emphasizing psychological processes over biological
differences. The study attempts to distinguish "real" from imposed, or constructed, differences and includes reviews of various theories on their origins.
"Summary and Commentary" categorizes theories on differences as "un-
founded" (such as the notion that boys are more analytical than girls), "fairly
well established" (such as the idea that girls have greater verbal ability than
boys), and "open questions" (such as the theories on tactile sensitivity).
Discusses implications for social issues like schooling, child-care. Tables.
Comprehensive annotated bibliography of research studies on sex differences.

Mitchell, Juliet, and Jacqueline Rose, eds. *Feminine Sexuality: Jacques Lacan and the École Freudienne*. Translated by Jacqueline Rose. London: Macmillan, 1982. Reprint. New York: W. W. Norton, 1985.

Collection of major essays on female sexuality by one of Freud's most important revisers, a maverick French psychoanalyst who has become both extremely influential and very controversial among recent feminist theorists. The essays, all of them dense and difficult, include "The Meaning of the Phallus" (proposing the phallus as culture's main signifier) and "Feminine Sexuality in Psychoanalytic Doctrine." An introduction by Mitchell traces Freudian theory, responses to it, and Lacan's place in contemporary psychoanalytic theory. Rose's introduction discusses Lacanian texts, offering cogent explanations of extremely complex theories on identity and female sexuality. Figures. Bibliography.

Quinn, Susan. *A Mind of Her Own: The Life of Karen Horney*. New York: Summit Books, 1987.

Biography of a psychoanalyst (1885-1952) who challenged Freud's theories about women, particularly his ideas about female sexual development. Quinn describes Horney's conflicts with Freud, centering on Horney's thesis that women's penis envy and castration complex could lead to a retreat from femininity and identification with the unattainable father, rather than the traditional Freudian idea that such complexes lead to the desire for a baby and the acceptance of femininity. Illustrations. Bibliographic essay.

Sagan, Eli. *Freud, Women, and Morality: The Psychology of Good and Evil*. New York: Basic Books, 1988.

A critique of Freudian theories on the development of the moral sense, including the idea that women have a weaker superego and therefore a less highly developed sense of justice. Sagan proposes "conscience" as a substitute for the superego, developing from the basic nurturing relationship between mother and child. Thus he argues that women are the source of morality.

Storr, Anthony, ed. *The Essential Jung*. Princeton, N.J.: Princeton University Press, 1983.

Selections from the basic writings by psychological theorist Carl Jung. Excerpts include sections of "The Relations Between the Ego and the Unconscious," which proposes the notion of "animus" and "anima"—psychic manifestations of "masculine" and "feminine" qualities respectively—as representatives of the persona in dreams.

Strouse, Jean, ed. *Women and Analysis: Dialogues on Psychoanalytic Views of Femininity*. New York: Grossman, 1974.

Reprints of basic writings by Freud, Karl Abraham, Helene Deutsch, Erik Erikson, and other theorists, paired with critiques and responses by Juliet Mitchell, Robert Coles, Margaret Mead, and others. The collection is very useful as a compendium of standard views and critiques. Includes Freud's major essays on female sexuality and Erikson's 1968 "Womanhood and the Inner Space" and his own response to feminist critiques of it. Editor's introduction traces psychoanalytic theories of female psychology from Freud to recent feminist analyses.

Williams, Juanita H., ed. *Psychology of Women: Selected Readings*. New York: W. W. Norton, 1979.
A collection of widely ranging source readings on women and psychology, grouped into sections by theme. Selections address myths and stereotypes, psychoanalysis, biology and behavior, sex differences, learning sex roles, sexuality, birth control, pregnancy and childbirth, changing life-styles, "deviance," and aging. Includes writings by the shapers of traditional psychology and related fields — Freud, Margaret Mead, Karen Horney, Erik Erikson — and feminist and other responses by people such as Adrienne Rich, Ruth Bleier, and Susan Sontag. Several essays address the lesbian experience, race, and cross-cultural comparisons. Each section has an introduction. Figures, tables.

Feminist Responses, Critiques, and Theories

Belenky, Mary Field, Blyth McVicker Clinchy, Nancy Rule Goldberger, and Jill Mattuck Tarule. *Women's Ways of Knowing: The Development of Self, Voice, and Mind*. New York: Basic Books, 1986.
A study that attempts to explain why women are at odds with traditional (that is, "male") ways of knowing. Authors argue that our culture's dependence on notions of objectivity as the source of knowledge leaves women silent and voiceless. Using extensive interviews and questionnaires, and basing their interpretation on theories like Carol Gilligan's idea of a "different voice," the authors look for women's experience of "voice." They emphasize their interviewees' use of subjective knowledge with the aim of developing a system of education that will further women's "connected knowing" and teaching. Includes women's accounts of experiences of college and academic life. Reference list. Appendix includes questionnaire.

Boston Lesbian Psychologies Collective, eds. *Lesbian Psychologies: Explorations and Challenges*. Urbana: University of Illinois Press, 1987.
Collection of articles on lesbian identity, sexuality, relationships with families and partners, and lesbians in therapy and in the community. Emphasizes a feminist perspective and the importance of revising traditional psychological

views of lesbians. Although essays focus on interpersonal dynamics rather than larger social forces, the book advocates a lesbian psychology that incorporates feminist analysis and "lesbian-affirming clinical orientations."

Chesler, Phyllis. *Women and Madness*. Garden City, N.Y.: Doubleday, 1972.
Early and influential feminist account arguing that social restrictions and tradi-tional sex roles lead to a response culturally defined as "mental illness" in women. Chesler uses examples from myth, art, and literature and draws heav-ily on interviews with women about their experiences of therapy and institu-tionalization. Includes chapters on mistreatment of women patients, including sexual abuse, and experiences of lesbians, Third World women, and feminists. The conclusion suggests the possibilities of feminist therapies. An appendix, "The Female Career as a Psychiatric Patient," provides data on sex, race, class, and marital statuses of patients in treatment from 1950 to 1969. Figures, tables, illustrations.

Chodorow, Nancy. *The Reproduction of Mothering: Psychoanalysis and the Sociol-ogy of Gender*. Berkeley: University of California Press, 1978.
Influential scholarly analysis of the effects of exclusive mothering by women, revising Freudian theories from a feminist perspective. Chodorow argues that the mother-child bond shapes boys' and girls' psyches differently, one result being close ties between women later in life. This "reproduces" mothering by developing girls' nurturance and their ability to form intimate ties and close bonds with others. Chodorow claims that equal parenting by men and women would improve culture's gender dynamics.

Dinnerstein, Dorothy. *The Mermaid and the Minotaur: Sexual Arrangements and Human Malaise*. New York: Harper & Row, 1976.
Dinnerstein claims that the sex roles mandated by culture perpetuate them-selves through childrearing practices, particularly women's primary respon-sibility for children. (When children reject authority figures in order to develop as independent beings, their rejection takes the form of woman-hating because of women's exclusive identification with the parental role.) She argues that changes in those practices—especially greater male participation—would help undermine other divisions between men and women and would end the "malaise" she sees among humans.

Friedan, Betty. "The Sexual Solipsism of Sigmund Freud." In her *The Feminine Mystique*. New York: W. W. Norton, 1963. Reprint. New York: Dell Books, 1970.
One of the first feminist critiques of Freud in the modern movement, part of one of the most influential analyses of women's position of the 1960's. Friedan argues that Freudian theory is at the root of women's oppression, and that his

theories—based on the behavior of Victorian women—are completely inapplicable to modern women. She demonstrates the extent to which popularizations of concepts such as penis envy and the castration complex have entered American culture, arguing that they are now so influential that it is almost impossible for women to question these ideas.

Gallop, Jane. *The Daughter's Seduction: Feminism and Psychoanalysis*. Ithaca, N.Y.: Cornell University Press, 1982.
Sophisticated and provocative theoretical discussion of psychoanalytic theory, its relation to feminism, and its role as a potential resource. Gallop takes off from Juliet Mitchell's research, with an emphasis on French theory— particularly that of Jacques Lacan but also that of French feminist writers such as Luce Irigaray, Hélène Cixous, and Catherine Clément. Includes readings of Freud's case study of "Dora."

Gilligan, Carol. *In a Different Voice: Psychological Theory and Women's Development*. Cambridge, Mass.: Harvard University Press, 1982.
Controversial feminist analysis of women's psychology. Gilligan argues that women base moral decisions on an ethic of care, while men base them on abstract justice. Much of this book's importance lies in the responses it has aroused, with critics claiming that Gilligan's sample is too small and that her thesis rests on questionable assumptions. Others see it as an important way of championing values traditionally held by women and overcoming Western culture's dehumanizing emphasis on competition and other "masculine" values.

Lauter, Estella, and Carol Schreier Rupprecht, eds. *Feminist Archetypal Theory: Interdisciplinary Re-Visions of Jungian Thought*. Knoxville: University of Tennessee Press, 1985.
Feminist essays revising Jung's theory of archetypes (recurring images in culture and the unconscious, with dreams providing access to a "self-portrait" of the psyche), applied here to religion, literature and other arts, and myth. Editors' introduction reviews Jung, the development of archetypal theory, and its usefulness to feminist theory, with archetypes defined as a feminist tool for examining patterns in women's experience. Editors' theoretical conclusion argues that archetypes are an important basis for feminist theory because Jung's notion of the collective unconscious can lead to a collective consciousness and social change. Illustrations.

Miller, Jean Baker. *Toward a New Psychology of Women*. Boston: Beacon Press, 1976, 2d ed. 1986.
Influential examination of female psychology, stressing women's subordinate social position. Miller argues that conflicts between unequals lead members of

the subordinate group (here, women) to develop indirect ways of behaving. Describes the impact of subordination on thought processes and ways of conceptualizing, emphasizing the importance of women beginning with their own experience rather than rules of subordination and accepting conflict as a "basic process." Second edition updates original, with new foreword describing social changes and responses to the book.

Mitchell, Juliet. *Psychoanalysis and Feminism: Freud, Reich, Laing, and Women.* New York: Pantheon Books, 1974. Reprint. New York: Vintage Books, 1975.
One of the first serious attempts to reclaim Freudian theory for feminism, arguing that it provides the best explanation of how human psychology is shaped to fit "male" and "female" roles and how humans become men or women. Includes analyses and critiques of earlier feminist attacks on Freud, which Mitchell claims are based on feminist critics' refusal to accept the existence of the unconscious mind. An influential work which anticipates much recent feminist appropriation of Freudian, Lacanian, and other psychoanalytic theory.

Sayers, Janet. *Sexual Contradictions: Psychology, Psychoanalysis, and Feminism.* New York: Tavistock Publications, 1986.
A sophisticated review and critique of standard psychological theories— including post-Freudians theories (with chapters on Melanie Klein and Jacques Lacan), biological determinism, cognitive-developmental theory, and object relations theory. Analyzes the "psychology of men's social dominance and women's resistance to it," arguing for the relevance of Freud because his theories deal with contradictions. The final section outlines clinical approaches, including discussion of Freudian case studies. Sayers stresses the importance of dealing with both women's oppression and their resistance to it. She concludes that feminism must move beyond psychoanalysis' focus on individual suffering. Illustrations. Reference list.

Scarborough, Elizabeth, and Laurel Furumoto. *Untold Lives: The First Generation of American Women Psychologists.* New York: Columbia University Press, 1987.
History and collective biography of the first women in American psychology. The authors focus on the lives and contributions of individual women and of women psychologists as a group in order to explain why they have been excluded from the official history of the discipline. Introduction outlines context of women's entry into the field, including development of psychology as a profession; conclusion brings experience of women in psychology up to the late 1980's. Chapters draw extensively on personal writings of the women described. Illustrations. Appendices provide "cameo portraits" of additional women, published sources. References include manuscript collections.

Tavris, Carol, and Carole Offin. "Freud, Fantasy, and the Fear of Woman: The Psychoanalytic Perspective." In their *The Longest War: Sex Differences in Perspective*. New York: Harcourt Brace Jovanovich, 1977, reprint 1984.

Brief summary and critique of psychoanalytic theories about femininity and female sexuality. Includes a discussion of Freud and other psychoanalysts. Tavris and Offin's criticism is based largely in non-Freudian psychological theory and social science research techniques (such as the lack of random sampling in Freud's work).

Walsh, Mary Roth, ed. *The Psychology of Women: Ongoing Debates*. New Haven, Conn.: Yale University Press, 1987.

Paired essays debating variety of issues—including the relevance of psychoanalysis to women, the psychological impact of physiology, women and success, the idea of androgyny, the influence of sex differences on achievement and judgment, whether lesbianism should be defined as a "sickness," and the impact of abortion and pornography on women. Editor's introduction traces the history and development of debates on the psychology of women. Contributors include Sandra Lipsitz Bem, Carol Gilligan, Nancy Chodorow, Katharina Dalton, Alice Rossi, and Charles Socarides. Figures. Name and subject indexes.

Weitz, Shirley. *Sex Roles: Biology, Psychology, and Social Foundations*. New York: Oxford University Press, 1977.

Examination of the bases of contemporary sex roles from a social psychology perspective, emphasizing the interaction between psychological, biological, and social "maintenance systems." Weitz explores psychological means of socialization into conventional gender identities and argues that masculine and feminine cannot be separated or understood alone. Book includes cross-cultural comparisons between the United States and the Soviet Union, Sweden, China, Israel.

VIOLENCE AGAINST WOMEN

Rape

Bart, Pauline B., and Patricia H. O'Brien. *Stopping Rape: Successful Survival Strategies*. Elmsford, N.Y.: Pergamon Press, 1985.
Study of women's successful strategies for resisting and avoiding rape, based on extensive interviews. Contains a chapter correlating avoidance and women's ethnicity and a chapter on "Why Men Rape," which includes a discussion of men's misinterpretation of women's behavior. Appendices include analyses of the survey sample, self-report questionnaire, and a case transcript. Bibliography and case and subject indexes.

Brownmiller, Susan. *Against Our Will: Men, Women and Rape*. New York: Simon & Schuster, 1975.
Classic feminist analysis of rape. Brownmiller argues that rape is a logical extension of cultural attitudes toward male sexuality, including the idea that men's sexual desires are uncontrollable. One of the first full-length examinations of rape from a feminist perspective, crucial in shaping subsequent views.

Davis, Angela Y. "Rape, Racism, and the Myth of the Black Rapist." In her *Women, Race, and Class*. New York: Random House, 1981. Reprint. New York: Vintage Books, 1983.
As part of her larger analysis of racism, Davis argues that the rhetoric of feminist anti-rape literature depends on racist assumptions, including white women's fears of black men. Her critique focuses specifically on Brownmiller's *Against Our Will*.

Estrich, Susan. *Real Rape: How the Legal System Victimizes Women Who Say No*. Cambridge, Mass.: Harvard University Press, 1987.
The author, a lawyer and professor of criminal law, begins her examination of the legal system's treatment of rape with an account of her own experience of rape. The book emphasizes the system's inability to deal with anything beyond the "classic" aggravated rape (violent assault by a stranger) and analyzes individual cases, legal precedents, jury reactions, and other evidence of legal responses to "simple" rape (which includes acquaintance rape and cases not involving overt violence). Ends with a call for society's serious condemnation of all forms of coercive sex, insisting that "simple rape is real rape."

Griffin, Susan. "Rape: The All-American Crime." In *Women: A Feminist Perspective*, edited by Jo Freeman. Palo Alto, Calif.: Mayfield, 1975.
Discussion of the prevalence of rape in the United States, examining women's

experience and fears. Surveys beliefs and myths (for example, that women enjoy force) versus facts, suggesting that only a "quantitative difference" may separate a rapist from a normal heterosexual man—with rape located on continuum of male behavior. Includes details of a rape trial, emphasizing the widely divergent legal attitudes toward the sexual histories of the victim and the accused rapist. Equates rape with white men's treatment of blacks, "rape" of earth, Vietnam War.

Herman, Dianne. "The Rape Culture." In *Women: A Feminist Perspective*, edited by Jo Freeman. 3d ed. Palo Alto, Calif.: Mayfield, 1984.
Herman critiques traditional studies of rape that assume that male sexuality is inherently violent and aggressive and attacks rape laws protecting women as men's property. Analyzes myths, police response, and judicial procedures. Argues that "in a rape culture even the victims believe that men are naturally sexually aggressive," an attitude which puts burden on women to avoid rape.

Russell, Diana E. H. *The Politics of Rape: The Victim's Perspective*. New York: Stein & Day, 1975.
Based on a study of rape victims, this book's chapters consist largely of interviews with victims or rapists. Emphasis is on the victims' point of view and their interpretation of the experience of rape, including stranger and acquaintance rape. Russell examines rape's place in the larger society, including five chapters dealing with racism and two on the connection between rape and "mystiques" of masculinity and femininity. Conclusion describes strategies for preventing and dealing with rape, from self-defense and individual resistance to larger organizations and crisis centers. Advocates changes in criminal and judicial procedures and hospital treatment of victims. Appendix reprints "Rape Prevention Tactics and Advice on What to Do If You Are Raped," by Bay Area Women Against Rape. Bibliography.

——————— . *Rape in Marriage*. New York: Macmillan, 1982.
Groundbreaking examination of marital rape, based on a four-year study—the first to provide data from a random sample of women—by an activist-researcher influential in changing the definition of marital rape as a crime. Russell locates marital rape along a continuum of other sexual behavior and forms of abuse, drawing on lengthy excerpts from wives' accounts of incidents. Examines the attitudes of both partners, including questions about why women stay in such marriages, and includes chapters on wife-murder ("femicide") and international perspectives. Appendices describe several prosecutions against husbands and list state-by-state information on marital rape exemption laws. Bibliography.

Stanko, Elizabeth A. *Intimate Intrusions: Women's Experience of Male Violence*. Boston: Routledge & Kegan Paul, 1985.

An examination of all forms of violence by men against women—"men's threatening, intimidating and violent behaviour"—including rape, murder, incest, wife abuse, and sexual harassment, in Great Britain and the United States. Stanko discusses women's survival strategies (particularly ways of avoiding male violence), arguing that the fear of real and potential victimization defines women's experience in most male-dominated cultures. Includes personal accounts from a variety of sources and a discussion of responses and attitudes of officials, police, lawyers, prosecutors, and others. Concluding chapter calls for women to protest and organize against violence. Figures. Bibliography.

Tomaselli, Sylvana, and Roy Porter, eds. *Rape*. New York: Basil Blackwell, 1986.
Essays on rape from the standpoints of various disciplines—including law, philosophy, psychoanalysis, biology, art criticism, and history. The collection is meant to provide a "backdrop" for further research and analysis. Tomaselli's introduction discusses the possibilities of a future free of rape and reviews changing cultural attitudes toward rape from classical myth onward. Contributors address law reforms; configurations of rape in Greek myth, visual arts, and stereotypes of the rapist in popular culture; and the historical meanings of rape. Anthropologist Peggy Reeves Sanday's "Rape and the Silencing of the Feminine" provides a cross-cultural consideration. Illustrations.

Tower, Cynthia Crosson. *Secret Scars: A Guide for Survivors of Child Sexual Abuse*. New York: Viking Penguin, 1988.
An introduction to the subject of child sexual abuse, directed mainly at victims, family members, and therapists but providing useful background information for general readers. The book's focus is on the victim's feelings, including guilt, fear, and confusion, with an emphasis on survival and recovery. Appendix includes reading lists and state-by-state and Canadian resources for information and survivors' networks.

Warshaw, Robin. *I Never Called It Rape: The Ms. Report on Recognizing, Fighting, and Surviving Date and Acquaintance Rape*. New York: Harper & Row, 1988.
Based on a major study of sexual assault, chapters address definitions of date and acquaintance rape, the perspectives of victims and perpetrators, possible explanations for assaults, and their aftermath, including police and other institutional responses, prevention, survival, and recovery strategies. Includes a chapter on how men can work to stop acquaintance rape and many excerpts from first-person accounts. An afterword by May P. Koss, M.D., describes methods used in compiling a related study on campus sexual assault. Bibliography, resource list.

Domestic Violence and Incest

Armstrong, Louise. *The Home Front: Notes from the Family War Zone*. New York: McGraw-Hill, 1983.

Incest survivor Armstrong considers family violence (including incest) and the cultural response to its recent "discovery." Using the image of the family as a combat zone, she discusses the history and development of the juvenile justice system and family court, U.S. history of marital rape and incest, and the perception of perpetrators of domestic violence and incest as "sick" rather than criminal. One chapter is a case study of a child committed to a mental hospital without justification and later abused by a foster parent.

Browne, Angela. *When Battered Women Kill*. New York: Free Press, 1987.

Study of women who kill or attempt to kill battering husbands or lovers, based on extensive interviews with forty-two women in fifteen states. Lengthy excerpts from interviews are included in the text. Chapters trace the childhood backgrounds of the women interviewed, the development of the relationships and of violence within them, and the legal system's response to the women's reports of violence and to homicide. (The chapter on the legal system provides a good step-by-step explanation of women's process through it.) Browne emphasizes the importance of the larger cultural context, including the necessity of seeing men's abusive behavior within the context of romantic traditions that place men and women in particular roles. The study finds no significant difference between battered women who kill and those who do not but finds that the men involved drank more, used more drugs, and made more threats and assaults against women and children. Epilogue describes disposition of cases discussed. Appendix provides interview schedule. Case study, author, and subject indexes.

Fedders, Charlotte, and Laura Elliot. *Shattered Dreams: The Story of Charlotte Fedders*. New York: Harper & Row, 1987.

The biography—from childhood through divorce—of the abused wife in a highly publicized spouse-abuse case. Fedders was married to a prominent Washington lawyer, a high-powered overachiever and eventual chief of enforcement for the Securities and Exchange Commission. The account pays close attention to Fedders' Catholic faith, emphasizing the family's affluence, success, and the outward appearance of a perfect life in order to undermine the myth that domestic violence is confined to working-class or culturally disadvantaged families. Illustrations.

Fraser, Sylvia. *My Father's House: A Memoir of Incest and Healing*. New York: Ticknor & Fields, 1988.

Autobiographical account by Canadian journalist and novelist. Fraser describes her efforts to recall and deal with her childhood experience of incest—the memory of which she repressed completely until well into adulthood.

Giles-Sims, Jean. *Wife Battering: A Systems Approach*. New York: Guilford Press, 1983.

Sociological analysis of processes shaping the experiences of battered women, based on interviews with women seeking help at shelters. Study is written from the victims' perspective. Focuses on family structure, interactions between partners, patterns of behavior, and questions about why women stay in battering relationships. Includes three detailed case studies. Concludes with a six-stage general systems model for establishing patterns and explaining the behavior of both husbands and wives. Appendices describe research process and reprint interview questionnaires. Figures.

Gordon, Linda. *Heroes of Their Own Lives: The Politics and History of Family Violence, Boston 1880-1960*. New York: Viking Press, 1988.

The first comprehensive history of family violence, using social service agency documents to examine families' experience of domestic abuse and agencies' responses to it. Chapters discuss incest, child and spouse abuse, child neglect, and social policy. Gordon argues that women have often actively sought help from the agencies and helped to shape social workers' attitudes, rather than being simply passive victims of either abuse or social control. Although specific examples are limited to Boston, Gordon's thesis can be applied widely. Extensive examples from case histories are included. Illustrations, tables, figures. Appendices describe research and analytic methods and characteristics of clients discussed in study.

Hechler, David. *The Battle and the Backlash: The Child Sexual Abuse War*. Lexington, Mass.: Lexington Books/D. C. Heath, 1988.

An investigation of the controversy over recent cases of child sexual abuse, focusing on the struggle to bring attention to such abuse and the resulting "backlash"—claims that children and/or prosecutors have misrepresented the facts or falsely accused adults of sexual abuse. Includes detailed examinations of individual cases—including large-scale cases (as in day-care centers or schools) and those involving single victims, as well as those that have been both well publicized and unpublicized. Hechler's analysis draws on the views of professionals in the field and other experts on both sides of the issue, and addresses legal and policy questions, employing extensive quotes from interviews. The conclusion recommends standardized procedures for investigating charges of sexual abuse of children and urges evaluations of current programs, methods, and courtroom procedures. Hechler also argues in favor of public education about child sexual abuse and funding for victims' therapy regardless of court decisions in individual cases. Appendix provides lengthy excerpts from interviews with victims of sexual abuse.

Herman, Judith Lewis, with Lisa Hirschman. *Father-Daughter Incest*. Cambridge, Mass.: Harvard University Press, 1981.

A feminist analysis of father-daughter incest as a paradigm of female sexual victimization. The author argues that the victimized daughter represents women at their most powerless because the relationship between a father and daughter is so unequal and because the father's domination of the traditional family gives him the power to make sexual use of children. Includes discussion of questions of blame and harm; the dynamics of the incestuous family; the "crisis of disclosure"; and remedies, including criminal prosecution, therapy, and prevention. Stresses the importance of preventive education, necessary changes in the power structure of the family and women's status, including the integration of men into child care. Appendix, "The Incest Statutes," lists state-by-state laws.

Lystad, Mary, ed. *Violence in the Home: Interdisciplinary Perspectives*. New York: Brunner/Mazel, 1986.

Essays on family violence by psychiatrists, a social worker, a lawyer, researchers, and others. Essays are grouped into four sections: violence and American society, including an examination of the dynamics of violent families; social, structural, and psychological causes of family violence; clinical intervention programs for families and children; and community intervention programs, including prosecution. Editor's overview introduces issues and provides basic statistics. Violence is broadly defined to encompass all behavior involving physical aggression, with domestic violence described as a public health problem. Lystad calls for specific social policies, including substantial changes in social institutions; insists on the necessity of interdisciplinary research; and attacks media glorification of violence. Tables, figures, and an index.

Okun, Lewis. *Woman Abuse: Facts Replacing Myths*. Albany: State University of New York Press, 1986.

Study by a male counselor involved in the domestic violence movement. Okun begins with an extensive review and critique of the literature on domestic violence and then offers results of his study, based on interviews with women seeking help at a shelter and with male batterers in counseling. Among the factors considered for both victims and batterers are race, class, alcohol use, previous experience of abuse (including child abuse), education, and access to shelter or counseling. Conclusion analyzes the study, notes discrepancies between husbands' and wives' reports of incidents, and discusses implications of repeated separations and reconciliations. Tables. Appendices summarize sample variables and reprint shelter and counseling intake forms.

Pagelow, Mildred Daley, with Lloyd W. Pagelow. *Family Violence*. New York: Praeger, 1984.

120   *Women's Issues*

Extensive interdisciplinary examination of family violence—including wife
battering, abuse and neglect of children, incest, marital rape, and less discussed forms such as abuse of parents by children and battering of husbands.
Pagelow reviews a variety of theoretical approaches, treatments, and forms of
intervention; discusses pornography and family dynamics; and examines concepts such as the "cycle of abuse." Concludes with recommendations for
changes in laws and society, including elimination of overt social forms of
violence (extremely violent sports, child pornography, capital punishment), the
establishment of gun control laws, better social services, and education about
violence and family structures. Tables, illustrations. Appendix provides annotated bibliography on parenting. Lengthy reference list.

Rush, Florence. *The Best Kept Secret: Sexual Abuse of Children*. Introduction by
Susan Brownmiller. Englewood Cliffs, N.J.: Prentice-Hall, 1980.
One of the first comprehensive examinations of sexual abuse of children by a
major activist on behalf of victims. Rush considers incest and molestation by
friends, relatives, and strangers—with many examples based on personal accounts and interviews. Traces the tradition of child marriage and the history of
incest to the Bible and the Talmud. Explores Christian definitions, ancient
Greek tradition, myths and fairy tales, traditional Freudian interpretations of
incest and sexual abuse reports, and popular culture representations. Includes
discussions of laws, child prostitution, pornography, and abusive implications
of certain arguments for "liberated" sexuality. Rush concludes with a call for a
program of total re-education about the inevitably coercive nature of child-
adult sex.

Schechter, Susan. *Women and Male Violence: The Visions and Struggles of the
Battered Women's Movement*. Boston: South End Press, 1982.
History of the movement against domestic violence, from its origins in grass-
roots organizing with a base in the anti-rape movement through the development of shelters. Contains chapters on specific local and regional examples
(Massachusetts, Pennsylvania, New York City) and national and international
movements. Schechter examines reforms in judicial systems and changes in
legislation. Includes chapters analyzing sources of family violence, the future
agenda for the movement, and organizing in the 1980's in the light of New
Right influence and funding cuts. Includes accounts by organizers and activists. Appendix reprints a public statement by Schechter, opposing the combination of services for women and children and arguing for a continued focus
on women as primary victims of spouse abuse. Bibliography and resource and
organization lists.

Stacey, William, and Anson Shupe. *The Family Secret: Domestic Violence in America*. Boston: Beacon Press, 1983.

Dallas, Texas, study based on hundreds of detailed case studies and interviews with women seeking help from hotlines and with professionals and experts. Chapters examine violence against women and children, men as perpetrators of domestic violence, women's options for dealing with abuse (including shelters), and legal possibilities (including the inadequacies of current laws). Authors argue that both the public and legislators need to be educated about the extent and significance of domestic violence and the need for intervention and funding of services. Study criticizes the "cult of violence," the cultural trend toward accepting extreme forms of violence (including media images). Includes lengthy quotations from victims and experts. Appendix summarizes study's statistics in tables and provides a "Severity Index" for measuring abuse. Selected bibliography.

Steinmetz, Suzanne K., and Murray A. Straus, eds. *Violence in the Family*. New York: Dodd, Mead, 1975.
Collection of sociological analyses of family violence, including sections on spouse and kin violence, child abuse, and "the family as training ground for societal violence." Editors' introduction debunks standard myths and stereotypes (for example, that working-class families are more violent than middle-class ones), examines social origins of family violence, and discusses the family as a system. Editors introduce each section, and there are abstracts for each article. Collection includes James A. Michener's "The Kent State Four/ Should Have Studied More," about parental reactions to the 1970 Kent State killings; Bruno Bettelheim's "Children Should Learn About Violence"; and examinations of the relation between experiences of family violence and students' commitments to particular political views. Figures and tables. Subject and author indexes.

Straus, Murray A., Richard J. Gelles, and Suzanne K. Steinmetz. *Behind Closed Doors: Violence in the American Family*. Garden City, N.Y.: Anchor Press/ Doubleday, 1980. Reprint. Newbury Park, Calif.: Sage Publications, 1988.
First national study of domestic violence, including spouse battering, child abuse, and violence between siblings. Authors discuss social patterns, immediate causes, the future of family violence, and possible solutions. (Among immediate causes, the study lists stress arising from financial problems, family size, and various kinds of unresolved conflict.) Calls for additional shelters, provision of day care and improved child welfare services, and a rejection of social norms that permit and even glorify violence. Appendices describe the sample and interview techniques and provide indexes and scales for measuring violence, conflict, stress, and power within families. Charts.

Walker, Lenore E. *The Battered Woman*. New York: Harper & Row, 1979.
Based on interviews with battered women and the author's clinical practice as

a psychologist. The prologue is a personal account by a battered woman, and the text includes lengthy quotations throughout. The study is divided into sections on the psychology of battered women, coercive techniques in battering relationships, and "the way out" (including legal and social resources, shelters, and therapy). Attacks myths, especially that battered women are "masochists," and describes patterns.

Pornography

Copp, David, and Susan Wendell, eds. *Pornography and Censorship*. Buffalo, N.Y.: Prometheus Books, 1983.
Philosophical essays (on liberalism and pornography, art, and other subjects), social science studies (including empirical studies of men's and women's reactions), and legal briefs (from Great Britain and the United States) on issues of pornography and censorship. Copp's introduction examines the relationship between pornography and obscenity, recommending that pornography be defined as material containing obscenity that violates canonical norms. Discusses degrees of pornography, legal criteria, censorship and freedom of expression issues, and the problems involved in doing empirical research on pornography. The collection includes work by Diana E. H. Russell and Edward Donnerstein. Includes selected bibliographies on philosophical, social science, and legal studies.

Griffin, Susan. *Pornography and Silence: Culture's Revenge Against Nature*. New York: Harper & Row, 1981.
Analysis of pornography as a cultural force, arguing that, although often linked to the idea of sexual liberation, it is actually an expression of "a fear of bodily knowledge and a desire to silence eros." Griffin examines pornographic imagery (including examples from the seventeenth century), pointing out not only connections between pornography and violent ideologies such as Nazism and racism but also ties to what she sees as a culture-wide denigration and silencing of women's autonomous sexuality and identity.

Lederer, Laura, ed. *Take Back the Night: Women on Pornography*. New York: William Morrow, 1980.
Collection of essays against pornography from a feminist perspective, including essays by women who have participated in producing pornography and activists in other areas—along with perspectives from lesbians, black women, and women in other countries. The collection as a whole argues that the pornography industry exploits and abuses women and that feminists should make its abolition a top priority. Among contributors are Gloria Steinem, Helen Longino, Florence Rush, Alice Walker, and Andrea Dworkin. Afterword

by Adrienne Rich. Includes excerpt from Susan Brownmiller's *Against Our Will* and Audre Lorde's "Uses of the Erotic."

Malamuth, Neil M., and Edward Donnerstein, eds. *Pornography and Sexual Aggression*. Orlando, Fla.: Academic Press, 1984.
Collection of recent studies on effects of pornography, mostly focusing on experimental research involving responses to direct exposure and questions of sexual aggression. Introduction provides a historical perspective on pornography research. Essays explore possible statistical correlations between the availability and sale of pornography and violence against women (particularly rape). H. J. Eysenck's afterword, "Sex, Violence, and the Media: Where Do We Stand Now?" examines the significance of studies and experimental research and argues that the field is a real test of social science. Eysenck explores evidence for and defects in research that supports theories connecting pornography and sexual aggression, concluding that effects of media presentations of sex and violence are clear. Figures and tables. Author and subject indexes.

Willis, Ellen. "Feminism, Moralism, and Pornography." In *Powers of Desire: The Politics of Sexuality*, edited by Ann Snitow, Christine Stansell, and Sharon Thompson. New York: Monthly Review Press, 1983.
A feminist argument against the censorship of pornography. Willis considers why women find the critiques of pornography so compelling but disagrees with the analysis of pornography as predominantly violent, arguing that antipornography laws can too easily be used against feminists and other political groups.

RELIGION AND SPIRITUALITY

Women and Traditional Religions

Allen, Paula Gunn. "The Ways of Our Grandmothers." In her *The Sacred Hoop: Recovering the Feminine in American Indian Tradition.* Boston: Beacon Press, 1986.

Allen, a Native American poet and critic, considers female gods and women-centered rituals in the Native American spiritual tradition. The focus is on the effects of European colonization, with attention to both the continuation and the disruption of matriarchal traditions. The essays include descriptions of specific rituals and myths and Allen's recollections of her own education in the traditions.

Andolsen, Barbara Hilkert, Christine E. Gudorf, and Mary D. Pellauer, eds. *Women's Consciousness, Women's Conscience: A Reader in Feminist Ethics.* San Francisco: Harper & Row, 1985.

A collection of essays on feminist ethics, focusing on how social, cultural, and economic structures define dominant notions of ethical behavior and how women's experience within those structures can serve as a basis for a new kind of ethics. Contributors address a wide range of topics, but the majority of essays concentrate on religious experience, particularly women's position within traditional religions. Contents include discussions of women's unpaid labor, violence against women, feminism and peace, female friendship, anti-Semitism, black spirituality and sexuality, procreative choice, and a feminist theological critique of Christian ethics. The final section includes essays outlining and theorizing about the development of a feminist ethics. Contributors include many prominent feminist writers on religion and spirituality, among them Starhawk, June Jordan, Judith Plaskow, and Rosemary Radford Ruether.

Andrews, Lynn V. *Medicine Woman.* San Francisco: Harper & Row, 1981.

The first-person account of a woman's seven years of study with a Native American medicine woman, her initiation into rituals, and her mystical experiences. Illustrations.

Armstrong, Karen. *The Gospel According to Woman: Christianity's Creation of the Sex War in the West.* Garden City, N.Y.: Anchor Press/Doubleday, 1987.

A critical history of women in Christianity—both how men have regarded women and how women have attempted to live within the religion—by a former Anglican nun. Armstrong emphasizes both the damaging aspects of Christianity (Catholicism and Protestant denominations) and its positive influence on women's activism for social change. She argues that "women's main problem in the Western world has always been sex," and she considers various Christian "solutions," including Eve/witch images and the roles of virgin, martyr, and mystic. Draws on ancient theological writings and lives of women as different as Joan of Arc and Catharine Beecher.

Atkinson, Clarissa W., Constance H. Buchanan, and Margaret R. Miles, eds. *Immaculate and Powerful: The Female in Sacred Imagery and Social Reality*. Boston: Beacon Press, 1985.
Comparative and historical essays on women's place in religious tradition and symbolism. The collection covers a broad range of mainstream religions, including Hinduism, Judaism, Tibetan Buddhism, and various denominations of Christianity. Introduction by Miles emphasizes the importance of exploring the interface between religious symbols and social situations as a route to understanding both the creativity and the oppression of women. Argues that when oppressive religious myths—such as the limited views provided by the Eve/Mary dichotomy—are rejected, religion can be a powerful positive force in women's lives. Discusses the difficulty of using texts provided by men to understand women's experience. Essays address the history of women in ancient Israel, female sexuality in Hinduism, black women's literature and feminist theology, the nineteenth century Marian revival, and Simone Weil's religious imagery.

Beck, Evelyn Torton, ed. *Nice Jewish Girls: A Lesbian Anthology*. Trumansburg, N.Y.: Crossing Press, 1982.
Essays, personal narratives, and other accounts by and about Jewish lesbians. Although the collection focuses on lesbian experience, many essays deal directly with Judaism, including such topics as ethnic diversity among Jews, possible conflicts facing feminists and lesbians who identify themselves with Judaism, and strategies for reclaiming Jewish heritage.

Bullough, Vern L., Brenda Shelton, and Sarah Slavin. "Sex Is Not Enough: Women in Islam." In their *The Subordinated Sex: A History of Attitudes Toward Women*. Rev. ed. Athens: University of Georgia Press, 1988.
This chapter in a larger study of changing ideas about women describes Islam as "sex-positive"—that is, promoting positive attitudes toward sexuality and eroticism (as opposed to "sex-negative" Christianity)—but still misogynist. Includes history of Islam, beginning with the origins of its sexual attitudes, but emphasizes ideas about women and social institutions (such as the harem), drawing on the Koran, Muslim traditions, myths, and literature. The authors argue that Islamic women have historically had no autonomous institutions, only male-created myths, and that positive attitudes about sexuality do not necessarily mean positive attitudes toward women.

Carroll, Jackson W., Barbara Hargrove, and Adair T. Lummis. *Women of the Cloth: A New Opportunity for Churches*. San Francisco: Harper & Row, 1981.
Consideration of women's actual and potential role as Protestant clergy, based on extensive questionnaire and interviews of clerics, denominational officials, and seminary personnel. Includes a review of women's historical role in Protestant churches and their entry into the ministry. Chapters discuss family backgrounds of women clerics, their experiences at seminary, effectiveness of and attitudes toward male and female clergy, and the personal lives of ministers. Conclusions suggest that women clergy are competent but not always enthusiastically welcomed by laity. Appendix provides questionnaire and responses. Tables.

Christ, Carol P., and Judith Plaskow, eds. *Womanspirit Rising: A Feminist Reader in Religion*. San Francisco: Harper & Row, 1979.
Collection of feminist essays on women's place in traditional religions (especially Judaism and Christianity) and alternative possibilities. Contributors include prominent feminist theologians and writers on women's spirituality, among them Rosemary Radford Reuther, Mary Daly, Elaine Pagels, and Starhawk. Essays consider traditional theology's attitudes toward women, questions about what traditional religion can offer women, possible reconstructions of tradition (including examples of rewritten prayers and rituals), and the creation of new traditions (including reclaiming witchcraft and organizing spiritual rituals around menstruation). Introduction argues that the sexism of traditional religions does not eliminate the human need for ritual, symbol, and myth.

Coles, Robert. *Dorothy Day: A Radical Devotion*. Reading, Mass.: Addison-Wesley, 1987.
Biography of the radical Catholic journalist and activist in the Catholic Worker Movement (1897-1980), based on Coles's long friendship with her, formal interviews, and the reminiscences of friends. Includes discussion of her fifty years as a columnist for *Catholic Worker* newspaper, her work as the founder of halfway houses and soup kitchens, and her activism in the Civil Rights movement and on behalf of the poor and homeless.

Daly, Mary. *The Church and the Second Sex*. 2d ed. New York: Harper & Row, 1975.
Critique from within of sexism in the Roman Catholic Church, originally published in 1968. Drawing on Simone de Beauvoir's analysis in *The Second Sex*, Daly argues for the radical transformation of the "life-destroying" elements of Catholicism, including the Church's complicity in maintaining the secondary status of women in Catholic countries. Daly's new "post-Christian" introduction to the second edition rejects Christianity entirely and provides a

chapter-by-chapter critique of book. An important early work by one of the most influential feminist critics of traditional religion. Offers a chance to see how her ideas have changed over time.

Friedman, Lenore. *Meetings with Remarkable Women: Buddhist Teachers in America*. Boston: Shambhala, 1987.
Interviews with seventeen women teaching Buddhism in the United States. Explores their commitment to the religion and way of life (including conversion from other traditions), the role of women in Buddhism, and the potential impact of women's greater presence at the level of teacher. Friedman's introduction reviews the history of women's involvement in Buddhism—both as devotees and as goddesses. Illustrations. Glossary of terms used in Buddhism. Appendix of useful addresses.

Griffin, Mary. *The Courage to Choose: An American Nun's Story*. Boston: Little, Brown, 1975.
Autobiography of a former nun, from Catholic girlhood to her decision to leave the convent. Includes a discussion of her choice to enter orders; her experiences as a nun, with an emphasis on women's role in Catholic Church and the details of daily life and training; the impact of Vatican II; and Griffin's growing involvement with the outside world, including the influence of the women's movement and feminist critiques of Catholicism. The last chapter speculates on the future of the religious life, including a description of new alternative religious communities.

Haddad, Yvonne Yazbeck, and Ellison Banks Findly, eds. *Women, Religion, and Social Change*. Albany: State University of New York Press, 1985.
Essays on women and the formation of religious tradition; social change and women's role in traditional religious institutions; and women, religion, and revolution around the world and specifically in North America. The collection includes both historical and contemporary examples and deals with Christianity, Judaism, Islam, Buddhism, and Hinduism. Nancy Falk's introduction points out structural parallels between religion and revolutionary movements (for instance, the Marxist "class struggle" as a reworking of the battle between good and evil). Collection includes essays on the role of women in the development of Buddhism; images of women in Islamic and Christian art, Hindu symbolism, and early Chinese Buddhism; religious aspects of women's role in the Nicaraguan revolution; and the relationship between religion and the American abolition movement. Index.

Heschel, Susannah, ed. *On Being a Jewish Feminist: A Reader*. New York: Schocken Books, 1983.
Essays on conflicts and tensions between Judaism and feminism, emphasizing

the possibility of remaining within traditional religion but "creating a feminist theology of Judaism." Essays explore women's place in Jewish texts, rituals, and family; stereotypes and realities of Jewish family life; and integrating ethnic, sexual, and religious identity with feminist ideals. Editor's introductions to book and individual sections review feminist critiques of Judaism. Glossary.

Hurcombe, Linda, ed. *Sex and God: Some Varieties of Women's Religious Experience*. New York: Routledge & Kegan Paul, 1987.
Essays, personal accounts, stories, and poetry by women on spirituality and religion, focusing on the Judeo-Christian tradition. Contributors include peace activist Starhawk, theologian Rosemary Radford Ruether, writers Susan Griffin and Sara Maitland. Collection emphasizes the integration of sexuality and spirituality but also examines women's place in traditional and alternative religions and rituals, including "reformist" approaches to mainstream denominations. Includes an essay on "choosing celibacy as a nun."

James, Janet Wilson, ed. *Women in American Religion*. Philadelphia: University of Pennsylvania Press, 1980.
Collection of essays on women's role in American religion from the Colonial period to the 1950's, including a variety of denominations (Quaker, Congregationalist, Evangelical groups, Catholic, Jewish, Lutheran). Editor's "Women in American Religious History" provides overview; other essays examine the participation of women as missionaries, nuns, family members, and parishioners.

Johnson, Sonia. *From Housewife to Heretic*. New York: Doubleday, 1981.
Memoirs of a woman excommunicated from the Mormon Church for her support of the ERA. Johnson, now a prominent feminist, former Presidential candidate, and promoter of nontraditional women's spirituality, describes her growth from housewife to political activist and other women's responses to her situation.

King, Ursula, ed. *Women in the World's Religions, Past and Present*. New York: Paragon House, 1987.
Essays on women's position in religions around the world— including early goddess worship, traditional African religions, the Unification Church, Buddhism, the Hare Krishna movement, varied denominations of Christianity, and Judeo-Christian tradition generally. Contributions are grouped into sections on historic and systematic perspectives, contemporary perspectives, and feminist reflections, each introduced by the editor. Writers are working from within and outside the religions they discuss, and essays consider issues from the ordination of women in mainstream Christian denominations to women in the sym-

bolism and ritual of the Unification Church. Includes essay by King on "feminism and the transformation of religious consciousness." Index.

Koltun, Elizabeth, ed. *The Jewish Woman: New Perspectives*. New York: Schocken Books, 1976.

Essays on women and Judaism by women and men, including Carol Christ, Judith Plaskow, and Pauline Bart. Contributors examine issues of identity, history (including essays on Jewish feminists of past), life-cycle rituals, education, and holiday observations and ceremonies. Includes essays on women in Jewish law, women in Jewish literature from the Torah to contemporary fiction, and "The Jewish Women's Haggadah," by Aviva Cantor Zuckoff. Selected bibliography.

Lack, Roslyn. *Women and Judaism: Myth, History, and Struggle*. Garden City, N.Y.: Doubleday, 1980.

Analysis and critique of Jewish attitudes toward women, women's role in Jewish ritual, and Old Testament images and symbols. Accounts include the author's personal experiences, discussions of stereotypes of Jewish women, and individual chapters on Eve and Lilith. Lack deals with Reform, Conservative, and Orthodox denominations. The concluding chapter, "Unveilings," examines changes in the 1970's, especially the ordination of women as rabbis.

Marcus, Jacob Rader. *The American Jewish Woman: A Documentary History*. New York: KTAV Publishing, 1981.

Encyclopedic collection of documents, including autobiographical writings, poems, stories, newspaper accounts, and other excerpts describing Jewish women's experience in the United States from the eighteenth century to the modern age. Writings discuss family, business and work, money, politics, education, religion (including the ordination of women as rabbis), marriage and family, and social life. Illustrations.

Minai, Naila. *Women in Islam: Tradition and Transition in the Middle East*. New York: Seaview Books, 1981.

An examination of the changing role of women in Islam, focusing on the Middle East and North Africa. Written by a woman reared as a Muslim but with extensive Western experience, the work includes the history of women in Islam from early development of the religion to the present. Chapters on Islamic women across the life cycle (marriage, motherhood, widowhood), describing the experiences of individual women. Minai considers the impact of rapid Westernization, changes in socioeconomic background and culture, and the influence of feminism on Islamic attitudes toward women and on the women themselves. The conclusion discusses women and the Islamic revival, including Muslim women's experience and rejection of Western ideas and their view that Islam offers more (such as physical protection and financial support) than "liberation." Bibliography of English and foreign-language sources.

Mollenkott, Virginia Ramey, ed. *Women of Faith in Dialogue*. New York: Crossroad, 1987.
Short essays by women participating in Christian, Jewish, and Islamic denominations. Addresses struggles within their own religious communities and ways of working together for justice (including discussion of specific issues, such as anti-Semitism and nuclear war). Contributors include clergy, religious scholars, and scholars and writers in other fields. The collection assumes that, despite profound differences on some subjects, dialogue is possible because women share common experiences across traditions. Concludes with "Interreligious Worship Service," including an explanation of how to organize one. Appendix offers guidelines for forming a local group of women of faith.

Ochshorn, Judith. *The Female Experience and the Nature of the Divine*. Bloomington: Indiana University Press, 1981.
Analysis of gender and power in theology, comparing ancient polytheistic religions of Egypt, Mesopotamia, and Canaan with Old and New Testament and the Judeo-Christian belief systems. Ochshorn begins with questions about gender and theology and the nature of the divine, and her analysis includes the examination of texts and practices from both traditions. The epilogue describes the shift from polytheism to monotheism, in which men were defined as closer to and in special relationship to the deity, women more closely tied to material concerns. Ochshorn suggests that the importance of gender as a measure of individual worth may help explain the success of the Judeo-Christian system as a replacement for polytheistic traditions.

Preston, James J., ed. *Mother Worship: Theme and Variations*. Chapel Hill: University of North Carolina Press, 1982.
Essays examining female deities, with focus on "madonna complex" (worship of Virgin Mary) in Europe and Mexico and the persistence of Great Goddess worship in South Asia. Introductory essay discusses issues involved in cross-cultural study. Editor's conclusion surveys theories on mother worship from the nineteenth century to modern times, traces worldwide patterns, and examines the relationship between symbols of mothers and the "empirical cultural reality" of motherhood. Illustrations. Index.

Ruether, Rosemary Radford. *Women-Church: Theology and Practice of Feminist Liturgical Communities*. San Francisco: Harper & Row, 1985.
An effort by one of the most prominent Christian feminist theologians in the United States to reclaim religious tradition (focusing mainly on Christianity) for women by forming new communities of faith and ritual based in equality.

Within individual chapters, liturgies are presented for all aspects of women's lives: healing rituals after rape and incest, burglary, abortion, and miscarriage; coming-out rites for lesbians; covenant celebrations for heterosexual and lesbian couples; rituals to mark menstruation, menopause, and other life-cycle events; and celebrations of the year cycle. Includes bibliography of liturgies.

——————— , ed. *Religion and Sexism: Images of Woman in the Jewish and Christian Traditions*. New York: Simon & Schuster, 1974.
Essays on Jewish and Christian attitudes toward women. Includes discussion of images in the Old and New Testaments, the Talmud, and canon law; the role of women in the medieval church and the Protestant Reformation; and Judith Plaskow Goldenberg's "Epilogue: The Coming of Lilith," which imagines Adam's first wife returning to the Garden of Eden and joining forces with Eve. Patricia Martin Doyle's introductory essay on psychological and cultural implications argues that the image of women in traditional religion is "the single most important and radical question" in culture because of religion's profound effect on large numbers of people. Index.

Ruether, Rosemary Radford, and Eleanor McLaughlin, eds. *Women of Spirit: Female Leadership in the Jewish and Christian Traditions*. New York: Simon & Schuster, 1979.
Collection of essays on women as religious leaders, focusing mainly on women in Christian denominations. Contributors address history (including the early and medieval church, English Quakers' connections to radical politics, and Evangelical movements), changes in the experiences of American nuns, and the movement for ordination of women in the Episcopal and Roman Catholic churches. Editors' introduction argues against the idea—common to many feminist critics of mainstream religion—that heretical groups (such as witches) are more open to women leaders than traditional denominations. They do, however, find that religious orders, founding and renewal movements within Christianity, and denominations stressing lay leadership may have more space for women. Editors call for "radical obedience"—dissent from within traditional religions, rather than removal from them. Index.

Schlafly, Phyllis. *The Power of the Christian Woman*. Cincinnati: Standard Publishing, 1981.
Critique of feminism, arguing for the Christian woman's power based in adherence to biblical teachings and traditional Christianity. Schlafly rejects the idea of "gender-free equality" in favor of complementary male and female roles, arguing for the maintenance of the integrity of the traditional family. Book contains Schalfly's well-known attacks on the ERA and abortion. Appendices reproduce photographs of a pro-ERA march and the 1973 policy statement from the National Organization for Women.

Schneider, Susan Weidman. *Jewish and Female: Choices and Changes in Our Lives
    Today*. New York: Simon & Schuster, 1984.
    Encyclopedic discussion of issues confronting Jewish women, divided into
    sections on religious Judaism, relationships, and community. The emphasis is
    on reconciling Jewish identity and femaleness. Schneider assumes the pa-
    triarchal basis of traditional religions, seeing women as "disabled" Jews ex-
    cluded from many aspects of religious life, but is hopeful about the possibility
    of changing women's status and presents Judaism as already permanently
    transformed by women activists. Covers a wide range of topics, including
    history, law, religious observances, sexuality, family, marriage and divorce,
    community, and work. Includes valuable networking directory of organizations
    and resources for all areas of life, along with lists of resources throughout text.
    The book draws heavily on the personal experiences of Jewish women, includ-
    ing quotations. Illustrations.

Warner, Marina. *Alone of All Her Sex: The Myth and the Cult of the Virgin Mary*.
    New York: Alfred A. Knopf, 1976. Reprint. New York: Pocket Books, 1978.
    An analysis of the symbolic, cultural, and religious meanings of Mary, with an
    emphasis on her unique status in Catholic iconography. Chapters consider
    Mary as virgin, queen, bride, mother, and intercessor and trace the develop-
    ment of the figure as an idealization of womanhood and Eve's polar opposite,
    drawing on texts from the New Testament through twentieth century papal
    decrees. Epilogue argues that Mary is "the instrument of a dynamic argument
    from the Catholic Church about the structure of society." Illustrations. In-
    cludes a chronology of relevant historical events, arts and letters, and the
    development of Mariolatry.

Women-Centered Religions, Witchcraft, and Goddess Worship

Christ, Carol P. *Laughter of Aphrodite: Reflections on a Journey to the Goddess*.
    San Francisco: Harper & Row, 1987.
    Essays tracing the development of Christ's critique and ultimate rejection of
    the Judeo-Christian tradition as patriarchal and her embracing of ancient
    goddess-centered religion. Includes essays on theological and spiritual issues
    (such as "On Not Blaming Jews for the Death of the Goddess," a critique of
    implicit anti-Semitism in some analyses of the demise of goddess worship),
    and descriptions of visits to ancient Greek sites. Illustrations.

Daly, Mary. *Gyn/Ecology: The Metaethics of Radical Feminism*. Boston: Beacon
    Press, 1978.
    Radical feminist philosophy calling for the "exorcism of the internalized
    Godfather"—patriarchal habits and ways of thinking, typified by a male-

centered theology—and the reclaiming of a woman-centered worldview. Daly traces a metaphysical "journey" in which women repossess and celebrate names and images, processes, rituals, and ways of being that have been denigrated by patriarchal culture. The journey is emblematized by Daly's use of terms such as "crone" and "spinning," and although it draws heavily on goddess traditions, Daly's unique use of language sets her analysis apart from other approaches.

Sjoo, Monica, and Barbara Mor. *The Great Cosmic Mother: Rediscovering the Religion of the Earth*. San Francisco: Harper & Row, 1987.
Account of ancient woman-centered goddess worship, arguing that it is the original basis of contemporary traditional religions and was at the center of prehistoric women-oriented communities. The authors draw on theology, anthropology, political science, and other disciplines to trace the origins, flourishing, and demise of goddess worship. Includes section titled "Patriarchal Culture and Religion," with chapters on the development of male-centered religions and myths, the European witch-hunts, and critiques of Christianity. Illustrations. Bibliography and name and subject indexes.

Spretnak, Charlene, ed. *The Politics of Women's Spirituality: Essays on the Rise of Spiritual Power Within the Feminist Movement*. Garden City, N.Y.: Anchor Press/Doubleday, 1982.
Collection focusing exclusively on pre- and post-patriarchal, woman-centered spirituality (rather than critiquing traditional denominations), providing a useful introduction to the issues. Poems by prominent feminist writers (Judy Grahn, Adrienne Rich, June Jordan, Marge Piercy, Ntozake Shange) introduce sections on the history of women's spirituality, "manifesting personal power," and connections between the political and the spiritual. Contributors include Starhawk, Carol Christ, Mary Daly, Judy Chicago, Phyllis Chesler, Gloria Steinem, and Merlin Stone. Editor's introduction argues that traditional male-centered religions misrepresent women's nature and function. Calls for the recovery of women's spirituality as a feminist political force. Afterword demands rejection of patriarchal focus on conflict, alienation. Appendix describes two debates, one on hierarchy in women's spirituality, the other on whether the goddess and matriarchy are myth or reality. Bibliography.

Starhawk. *Dreaming the Dark: Magic, Sex, and Politics*. Boston: Beacon Press, 1982.
One of the most important promoters of witchcraft and feminist spirituality in the United States discusses the integration of the spiritual and the political, including pacifism and environmental movements. Starhawk calls for women to draw on "power-from-within" (versus "power-over," or domination), including the power of sexuality. (She defines "eros" as energy that demands a

nonhierarchical relationship to the sacred force, infusing even nonsexual tasks with erotic power.) Several chapters deal with facilitating groups, decision making, and dealing with conflict. Appendices provide history of witch-hunts, "Tools for Groups" (including aids to group rituals, questions for discussion), and chants and songs (with music).

_____ . *The Spiral Dance: A Rebirth of the Ancient Religion of the Great Goddess*. San Francisco: Harper & Row, 1979.
Collection of exercises, invocations, chants, rituals, spells, and myths for a return to ancient woman-centered spirituality. All are presented within a text that explains the history, philosophy, and details of witchcraft as a goddess-centered religion (as opposed to the popular view of witches), the oldest religion in the world. Includes "Tables of Correspondence."

Stone, Merlin. *Ancient Mirrors of Womanhood: A Treasury of Goddess and Heroine Lore from Around the World*. 2d ed. Boston: Beacon Press, 1984.
Collection of myths, stories, poems, and religious accounts centered on god-desses and strong women in ancient and traditional world religions. Includes examples from China and Japan, Latin America, Africa, Great Britain, the Middle East, Native American culture, India, Oceania, Scandinavia, and the Aegean. Introductions to each new culture, headnotes for each selection. Il-lustrations. Bibliography, list of woman-centered rituals and commemorations, "Astrological Considerations," index.

_____ . *When God Was a Woman*. New York: Harcourt Brace Jovanovich, 1978.
Influential history of early goddess-centered religions, their overthrow by men, and the rise of Judeo-Christian tradition as the root of male domination. Account draws on archaeology and other sources, urging women to search for their ancient heritage (not necessarily to return to ancient religion) and exam-ine the historical and political origins of the Bible. "Date Charts" provide chronologies of ancient cultures based on archaeological sites. Illustrations. Bibliography.

Walker, Barbara G. *The Woman's Encyclopedia of Myths and Secrets*. San Fran-cisco: Harper & Row, 1983.
Extensive encyclopedia of ideas, myths, events, people, and symbols related to women and religion, with an emphasis on women in ancient belief systems and in Judeo-Christian tradition. Focus is on the demise of organized goddess-worship and paganism and the persistence of related symbols and figures in Christianity through the Middle Ages. Brief introduction. Illustrations.

WOMEN AND THE ARTS

Visual Arts

Anscombe, Isabelle. *A Woman's Touch: Women in Design from 1860 to the Present Day*. New York: Viking Penguin, 1985.
History of women's contributions to design, focusing on modern house design and furnishings. The introduction provides an overview and traces that history from women's entry into the Arts and Crafts Movement to World War I. Chapters examine women designers by art-historical period, up to what Anscombe describes as the contemporary "return to 'normality.' " Includes discussions of individual women (such as Vanessa Bell), movements (Bauhaus, Russian design workshops), and the relationship of design to larger events and social changes. Covers all forms and genres, including pottery, textiles, furniture, decorative objects, and painting. Illustrations, including color plates. Chronology. Selected bibliography includes exhibit catalogs.

Bank, Mirra. *Anonymous Was a Woman*. New York: St. Martin's Press, 1979.
Anthology of women's traditional arts in the eighteenth and nineteenth centuries. Illustrations, including color plates, are matched with appropriate quotations from letters, autobiographical writings, advice books, and other contemporary sources. Includes wide range of arts and crafts, among them embroidery and other needle arts, quilts, tapestry, pastels, watercolors, and oils.

Broude, Norma, and Mary D. Garrard, eds. *Feminism and Art History: Questioning the Litany*. New York: Harper & Row, 1982.
Essays on feminism's challenge to art history. Introduction by editors argues that feminism readjusts one's historical perspective and therefore changes art history's view of all art. Includes essays on Classical, Dutch, German, and French art; medieval images of Eve and Mary; how the art history canon excludes some artists; and quilts, "the great American art." Illustrations. Index.

Chicago, Judy. *The Dinner Party: A Symbol of Our Heritage*. Garden City, N.Y.: Anchor Press/Doubleday, 1979.
Describes the making of Chicago's massive "Dinner Party" project, a collection of painted plates commemorating women and women's achievements. Includes photographs of the production process, color reproductions of plates, and short biographies of more than one thousand women represented on the plates and accompanying floor tiles.

Dewhurst, C. Kurt, Betty MacDowell, and Marsha MacDowell. *Artists in Aprons: Folk Art by American Women*. New York: E. P. Dutton, 1979.
A history of women without formal artistic training and, according to the authors, largely disregarded by art history. Discusses women whose artistic expressions included quilts, weaving, rugs, samplers, embroidery, and other needle arts; silhouettes, pottery, metalwork, and other decorative arts; and various forms of drawing and painting, including watercolors, portraits, and landscapes. Covers present-day artists working in folk traditions. Illustrations, including color plates. Brief biographies of the artists. Lengthy and useful bibliography organized by genre.

Greer, Germain. *The Obstacle Race: The Fortunes of Women Painters and Their Work*. New York: Farrar, Straus & Giroux, 1979.
Introductory history and analysis of women painters, with the emphasis on the social and cultural context. Greer's focus is on the obstacles to women artists' success and recognition, in opposition to the standard art history view of artists as isolated geniuses. Chapters consider those obstacles (including family, love, and how individual artists dealt with particular aesthetic issues) and how women confronted them (through, for example, specific genres of painting). The conclusion argues that women usually cannot become great artists because they are "damaged" by sexist society. Illustrations, including color plates.

Hale, Nancy. *Mary Cassatt*. New York: Doubleday, 1975.
Biography of the American woman painter (1844-1926), one of the most prominent Impressionists and the most important woman in the movement. Chapters address Cassatt's childhood, training and education, artistic influences, and friendship with Edgar Degas, emphasizing her struggle for recognition among male peers in the face of pervasive prejudice against women artists. Illustrations.

Harris, Ann Sutherland, and Linda Nochlin. *Women Artists: 1550-1950*. New York: Alfred A. Knopf, 1978.
Catalog of a Los Angeles County Museum of Art exhibition of European and American women painters. Introductory essays trace the history of women painters, pointing out both experiences and attitudes shared with male contemporaries and those common to women artists across time. (Harris covers the period from 1550 to 1800 and Nochlin covers post-French Revolution history.) Includes a discussion of issues related to "women's imagery." The catalog proper is composed of long entries on individual women, with biographical information and critical comments on paintings included in exhibit. Illustrations, including color plates. Individual artists' bibliographies, including lists of collections and exhibitions. General bibliography.

Hedges, Elaine, and Ingrid Wendt, eds. *In Her Own Image: Women Working in the Arts*. Old Westbury, N.Y.: Feminist Press, 1980.
Anthology of women's artistic creations, including both literature and visual arts. Sections address household work and women's art, obstacles and challenges to becoming an artist, "definitions and discoveries," and women's art and social change. Examples cover a wide range of creative expression, including work drawing on both traditional crafts and fine art traditions. Literary examples include poems, essays, and stories about art and women artists—all introduced by headnotes. Among literary contributors are Anne Bradstreet, Virginia Woolf, Alice Walker, Erica Jong, Elizabeth Barrett Browning, Adrienne Rich, and Lucille Clifton. Visual art—including paintings, sculpture, etchings, and drawings—is represented by illustrations, with explanatory headnotes. Among these contributors are Frida Kahlo, Marisol, and Judy Chicago.

Hess, Thomas B., and Elizabeth C. Baker. *Art and Sexual Politics: Women's Liberation, Women Artists, and Art History*. New York: Collier Books, 1973.
Reprints Linda Nochlin's famous essay, "Why Are There No Great Women Artists?"—one of the first feminist critiques of the artistic tradition and women's exclusion from it—and responses by ten women artists, including Louise Nevelson and Elaine de Kooning. Respondents both criticize and applaud Nochlin. Presents a range of attitudes on women as artists, the meaning of art, and women's position in general. Included are three other essays on related issues.

Lauter, Estella. *Women as Mythmakers: Poetry and Visual Arts by Twentieth-Century Women*. Bloomington: Indiana University Press, 1984.
A study of the ways that twentieth century women artists and poets transform negative myths about women in order to express female experience. Lauter draws on archetypal theories of mythmaking—including the work of Jung—and of feminist psychologists, literary critics, and art historians to describe women's mythmaking tradition, a process she sees as the result of a collective but not necessarily intentional vision. The conclusion argues that women artists and writers are moving away from traditional myths, a change that is suggested by their developing interest in goddess and matriarchal imagery, as well as artistic renderings of links between women and nature. She insists, however, that this is not the result of a "female brain" and instead uses the work of feminist psychologists such as Nancy Chodorow to argue that an understanding of women's absence of strong ego boundaries can be applied to women artists' visions of the boundaries between spirit and nature. Individual chapters address the work of visual artists Käthe Kollowitz, Remedios Varo, and Léonor Fini, and poets Anne Sexton, Margaret Atwood, and Diane Wakoski. Illustrations. Bibliography.

Lippard, Lucy R. *From the Center: Feminist Essays on Women's Art*. New York: E. P. Dutton, 1976.
   Influential essays by one of the most prominent American feminist art critics. Includes considerations of individual women artists (Judy Chicago, Eva Hesse, Louise Bourgeois, and others), women artists as a group, feminist art, and the films of Yvonne Rainer, Nancy Graves, Nancy Holt, and Rebecca Horn. "Free-lancing the Dragon" describes Lippard's efforts to become an art critic; "What Is Female Imagery?" consists of a discussion among Lippard, historian Linda Nochlin, painters Susan Hall and Joan Snyder, and architect Susan Torre. Also includes two fictional pieces. Illustrations, including color plates.

Munro, Eleanor. *Originals: American Women Artists*. New York: Simon & Schuster, 1979.
   Discussion of forty-four contemporary American women artists, drawing on interviews and combining biography, autobiography, and psychological pro-files. Introductory chapters review the position of women in contemporary art, consider how women artists face obstacles, describe women artists of last one hundred years, and profile Mary Cassatt and Georgia O'Keeffe as forerunners of contemporary artists. Illustrations, including excellent selection of color plates. "Selected Artists' Bibliography" includes catalogs.

O'Keeffe, Georgia. *Georgia O'Keeffe*. New York: Viking Press, 1976. Reprint. New York: Penguin Books, 1977.
   Catalog-style autobiography by one of the most important American women painters of the twentieth century, best known for her vivid flower paintings and landscapes of the American Southwest. O'Keeffe presents reminiscences and discussions of individual paintings, including their origins, to accompany color plates. The book begins with a memoir of childhood, early education and art training, and her first paintings. More than one hundred plates.

Parker, Roszika, and Griselda Pollock, eds. *Framing Feminisms: Art and the Women's Movement, 1970-1985*. New York: Routledge & Kegan Paul, 1987.
   Two long essays by Parker and Pollock (on feminist political strategies and the relationship between feminism and modernism) introduce a collection that documents the history of feminism and art since 1970. "Historical anthology" section includes reprints of articles, letters, handouts, and reviews of exhibits. The focus is British, but most issues also apply to U.S. artists and the Ameri-can women's movement. Introductions to each section. Illustrations.

Peterson, Karen, and J. J. Wilson. *Women Artists: Recognition and Reappraisal from the Early Middle Ages to the Twentieth Century*. New York: Harper & Row, 1976.
   Survey of women artists participating in the Western tradition, with individual

discussions of 150 women (some drawing on autobiographical writing). Sections are divided by historical era. Appendix on women artists of China. Illustrations. Bibliography. (A slide show is available to accompany text.)

Rubenstein, Charlotte Streifer. *American Women Artists: From Early Indian Times to the Present*. Boston: G. K. Hall, 1982.
Chronological survey of women artists in the United States. Introduction describes book's purpose as showing the relationship between women's art and their social and cultural circumstances. Sections provide overviews of each period, including discussions of dominant styles and genres, and entries on individual women working within and outside mainstream traditions. Long chapter on feminist art movement, including performance art; chapters on Native American artists, including twentieth century examples, and Chicana and Latina artists of the 1970's. Includes traditional fine arts (painting, sculpture, drawing), women's crafts (such as quilts), and nontraditional arts and materials. Illustrations, including color plates. Appendices present statistics on the representation of women artists in major national exhibitions, in institutions and academies, and among Guggenheim fellows.

Sherman, Claire Richter, ed., with Adele M. Holcomb. *Women as Interpreters of the Visual Arts, 1820-1979*. Westport, Conn.: Greenwood Press, 1981.
Essays on women as critics, historians, archaeologists, educators, curators, and administrators of art and art institutions. Editor's introductory chapters review some one hundred women artists and their contributions in a wide range of fields. Twelve bibliographic and critical essays discuss representative European and American women, grouped into nineteenth century women writers on art, late nineteenth and early twentieth century art historians and archaeologists, and contemporary scholars. Illustrations. Selected bibliography and index.

Slatkin, Wendy. *Women Artists in History: From Antiquity to the Twentieth Century*. Englewood Cliffs, N.J.: Prentice-Hall, 1985.
Introductory overview of the history of women painters, sculptors, and photographers. The book is divided by historical period, with discussions of individual women artists beginning in the Renaissance. The introduction addresses the relationship between art and the position of women in society, and each historical period is introduced by a survey of women's position. Includes brief sections on Afro-American artists and quilts. Illustrations. Bibliography.

Literature

Allen, Paula Gunn. "The Word Warriors." In her *The Sacred Hoop: Recovering the Feminine in American Indian Traditions*. Boston: Beacon Press, 1986.
These essays explore both traditional and contemporary literature, including

poetry by Native American women writers such as Leslie Marmon Silko. Allen argues that contemporary writers draw on oral traditions for themes, images, and worldview, and she traces some of the ideas (including attitudes toward spirituality) common to their work. An excellent introduction to the writing — particularly the poetry — of Native American women.

Bell, Roseanne P., Bettye J. Parker, and Beverly Guy-Sheftall, eds. *Sturdy Black Bridges: Visions of Black Women in Literature*. Garden City, N.Y.: Anchor Press/Doubleday, 1979.

Essays on literary portrayals of black women, including discussions of American, African, and Caribbean literature; works by women and men; and essays about individual writers and books and about larger genres. The collection includes considerations of black women as writers and as subjects of other people's writing, and is divided into three sections: critical and analytical essays, with discussions of Alice Walker, Zora Neale Hurston, and other writers; interviews and "conversations" with writers such as Ann Petry, Toni Cade Bambara, and Toni Morrison; and examples of imaginative writing by black women (among them Nikki Giovanni, Audre Lorde, and Paule Marshall). Also included are bibliographies on African-American, African, and Caribbean women writers. Illustrations.

DuPlessis, Rachel Blau. *Writing Beyond the Ending: Narrative Strategies of Twentieth-Century Women Writers*. Bloomington: Indiana University Press, 1985.

DuPlessis argues that women writers break the "scripts" of traditional narrative literature — including the quest and marriage plots — by imagining what might happen at some point beyond the conventional ending to those plots. Among others, she considers novelists Olive Schreiner and Virginia Woolf, poets Adrienne Rich, H. D., Denise Levertov, and Muriel Rukeyser. The final chapter addresses speculative fiction and the "collective protagonists" of writers such as Marge Piercy. A sophisticated argument, but not inaccessible to readers familiar with the writers under discussion.

Fetterley, Judith. *The Resisting Reader: A Feminist Approach to American Fiction*. Bloomington: Indiana University Press, 1978.

Critical analysis of selected classic works of American fiction by both women and men, describing the ways in which the texts depict women and issues of gender. Fetterley argues that women readers cope with the male-centered literary canon by "resisting" its message. Includes readings of "Rip Van Winkle," *A Farewell to Arms*, *The Great Gatsby*.

Gilbert, Sandra M., and Susan Gubar. *The Madwoman in the Attic: The Woman Writer and the Nineteenth-Century Imagination*. New Haven, Conn.: Yale University Press, 1979.

One of the most important feminist critical studies of the 1970's. Drawing on and revising Harold Bloom's theory of the "anxiety of influence," Gilbert and Gubar argue that nineteenth century women writers experienced an "anxiety of authorship"—the fear that they could not be writers because they could not follow male models—and expressed their anger through doubled characters. Sophisticated discussion of Jane Austen, Mary Shelley, Charlotte Brontë, George Eliot, and Emily Dickinson.

——————— , eds. *The Norton Anthology of Literature by Women: The Tradition in English*. New York: W. W. Norton, 1985.
Anthology of English-language fiction, drama, poetry, and essays by women, from the Middle Ages to the modern age. Each period and author is introduced by the editors, and the preface describes the collection as an attempt "to recover a long and often neglected literary history." Includes complete text of Charlotte Brontë's *Jane Eyre*. Selected bibliographies for each writer list primary and secondary sources.

Greene, Gayle, and Coppelia Kahn, eds. *Making a Difference: Feminist Literary Criticism*. New York: Methuen, 1985.
Collection of essays on feminist criticism, dealing with issues from language and psychoanalysis to sexuality, class, and race. Includes Bonnie Zimmerman's "What Has Never Been: An Overview of Lesbian Feminist Criticism," describing a tradition not only of criticism, but of lesbian literature. Index.

Hurston, Zora Neale. *Dust Tracks on a Road: An Autobiography*. Edited and introduced by Robert E. Hemenway. 2d ed. Urbana: University of Illinois Press, 1984.
Autobiography of the black novelist, folklorist, and cultural anthropologist. Hurston was an important figure in the Harlem Renaissance, a major collector of Afro-American and Afro-Caribbean folk tales, and is best known for her 1937 novel *Their Eyes Were Watching God*. Hurston discusses her Florida childhood, her family, her education (including her training as an anthropologist under Franz Boaz), and her collecting trips through the South and the Caribbean. Hemenway's introduction is a critical essay on Hurston, arguing that the book lacks a unified voice. Appendix provides chapters omitted from the original 1942 edition, including discussion of what Hurston calls "Race Pride," identifying it as a source of misunderstanding and injustice.

McCarthy, Mary. *How I Grew*. San Diego: Harcourt Brace Jovanovich, 1987.
Memoirs of the novelist and essayist, author of *Memoirs of a Catholic Girlhood* and *The Group*. Traces McCarthy's life from age thirteen (1925) to age twenty-one, from her childhood in Minneapolis through her years at Vassar

College, and includes reflections on the beginnings of her writing career. Illustrations. Supplemented by "Brief Biographical Glossary of Lesser-Known Figures," by Carol Brightman.

Millett, Kate. *Sexual Politics*. New York: Doubleday, 1969.
One of current feminism's first critical analyses of literature written by men, focusing on Norman Mailer, D. H. Lawrence, and others. Millett, who originally wrote the book as a dissertation in literature, attacks male writers' representation of women, particularly female sexuality, linking it to the oppressive "sexual politics" of the culture at large. Includes detailed readings of passages from individual novels.

Moers, Ellen. *Literary Women: The Great Writers*. New York: Anchor Press/ Doubleday, 1977.
One of the first major feminist surveys of women writers, focusing on nineteenth and twentieth century poets and novelists. Moers argues that, although women have been seen as secondary in the official literary tradition, they have developed an important tradition of their own, as well as a set of unique images and themes. Includes useful alphabetical guide to women writers and their work.

Nemiroff, Robert, ed. *To Be Young, Gifted, and Black: Lorraine Hansberry in Her Own Words*. Introduction by James Baldwin. Englewood Cliffs, N.J.: Prentice-Hall, 1969.
Letters, notes, essays, and play excerpts by one of the most important black women playwrights (1931-1965) in the United States, most famous for *A Raisin in the Sun* (1959). Includes writings on racial issues, the civil rights movement, and radical politics and a critical response to Norman Mailer's "The White Negro." Illustrations, including drawings by Hansberry.

O'Brien, Sharon. *Willa Cather: The Emerging Voice*. New York: Oxford University Press, 1987.
Critical biography of the novelist (1873-1947), focusing on her "apprenticeship"—the beginnings of her writing career, from childhood to the 1913 publication of *O Pioneers!* O'Brien traces the connections between Cather's life and her fiction, with an emphasis on the social and historical context, and presents her as a writer struggling to resolve culturally imposed contradictions between femininity and creativity. Includes discussion of Cather as a lesbian. Illustrations.

Olsen, Tillie. *Silences*. New York: Delacorte Press, 1978.
Series of reflections by short-story writer and novelist Olsen on the ways

women (and some men) writers are silenced and silence themselves. *Silences* was prompted by Olsen's own experience of a long interruption in her writing career.

Ostriker, Alicia Suskin. *Stealing the Language: The Emergence of Women's Poetry in America.* Boston: Beacon Press, 1986.
A history and critical discussion of U.S. women's poetry from 1650 to the present by an American poet and critic. Beginning with Anne Bradstreet (America's first published woman poet), Ostriker takes a feminist perspective on poetry and women writers, arguing that women's poetry has been ghettoized and denigrated by traditional critics, but that the details of such confinement have varied widely over the centuries. She views the history of women's poetry as a quest for autonomous self-definition and traces historical, stylistic, and thematic developments (such as the shift in the late 1960's and early 1970's from poetry about going mad to poetry critiquing male-dominated society). Dozens of poets are included, among them Adrienne Rich, Elizabeth Bishop, and Denise Levertov, as well as others far less famous. Lengthy bibliography lists works by women poets as well as critical studies.

Pratt, Annis V., with Barbara White, Andrea Lowenstein, and Mary Wyer. *Archetypal Patterns in Women's Fiction.* Bloomington: Indiana University Press, 1981.
Survey of more than three hundred novels and stories by women, with special attention to minor writers and their work. Pratt, an important practitioner of feminist archetypal criticism, argues that women's writing is linked by archetypes such as the "green world" of nature (a consolation for the problems of the real world), images of journeys, and rebirth and transformation—many of which are found in mythology and classical literature. Includes bibliography of novels and stories by women.

Rich, Adrienne. *On Lies, Secrets, and Silence: Selected Prose 1966-1978.* New York: W. W. Norton, 1979.
Essays by one of the foremost American poets. Many of them deal directly with writing, including reflections by Rich on her own writing experience ("When We Dead Awaken: Writing as Re-Vision"). Rich considers other women poets ("The Tensions of Anne Bradstreet," "Vesuvius at Home: The Power of Emily Dickinson") and works by women writers ("Jane Eyre: The Temptations of a Motherless Woman").

Russ, Joanna. *How to Suppress Women's Writing.* Austin: University of Texas Press, 1983.
Overview of responses to writing by women, describing the methods by which cultural and social forces—including publishers, critics, teachers, and other

purveyors of official culture—preserve literature as a male-centered domain. Includes discussions of major and minor women writers, written in science-fiction novelist Russ's irreverent style.

Showalter, Elaine. *A Literature of Their Own: British Women Novelists from Brontë to Lessing*. Princeton, N.J.: Princeton University Press, 1977.
Influential study of women novelists and a useful survey of writers, themes, and historical developments. Showalter describes and traces a tradition of women writing novels, including their reactions to and participation in the traditions defined by male writers. Includes consideration of the idea of a "female aesthetic" and analyses of a variety of genres (such as sensation novelists), writers dealing with specifically feminist issues, modernism, and contemporary novelists such as Doris Lessing and Margaret Drabble. "Biographical Appendix" presents chronological capsule biographies of dozens of women writers.

—————— , ed. *The New Feminist Criticism: Essays on Women, Literature, and Theory*. New York: Pantheon Books, 1985.
Anthology of feminist literary criticism, including essays by prominent American critics such as Showalter, Sandra Gilbert, Carolyn Heilbrun, and Rachel Blau DuPlessis. Reprints influential essays, among them Barbara Smith's 1977 "Toward a Black Feminist Criticism," which argues that the experience of black women readers and writers is excluded even from feminist criticism, and Annette Kolodny's 1980 "Dancing Through the Minefield: Some Observations on the Theory, Practice, and Politics of Feminist Literary Criticism," reviewing the "theoretical core" of the field. Editor's introduction surveys the development and impact of feminist criticism. Bibliography.

Sternburg, Janet, ed. *The Writer on Her Work*. New York: W. W. Norton, 1980.
A collection of essays by American women writers, including Anne Tyler, Mary Gordon, Alice Walker, Toni Cade Bambara, Susan Griffin, Erica Jong, Maxine Hong Kingston, and Muriel Rukeyser. Editor's introduction describes the difficulty of getting a clear view of women writers' experience, partly because of the lack of historical material but also perhaps because of writers' reluctance to tell all about their creativity. The essays themselves address personal and literary issues, particularly those concerned with being a woman writer, and range from explicit focuses on the larger social and historical contexts to highly personal reflections on individual writers' reasons for writing.

Stimpson, Catherine R. *Where the Meanings Are: Feminism and Cultural Spaces*. New York: Methuen, 1988.
A collection of essays by an influential feminist literary critic, selected from

her published work between 1970 and 1987. The collection includes essays on the connection between the women's liberation and black Civil Rights movements, the practice of women's studies, individual women writers (Tillie Olsen, Adrienne Rich, Virginia Woolf), the lesbian novel, and the relationship between feminism and feminist criticism. "Nancy Reagan Wears a Hat: Feminism and Its Cultural Consensus" (1987) surveys feminism's changing theories of culture and literary representation from the 1960's to the present, including a review of developing theoretical arguments about women's relationship to culture, literary texts, and representations of gender. Index.

Wagner-Martin, Linda. *Sylvia Plath: A Biography*. New York: Simon & Schuster, 1987.
Biography of the Pulitzer Prize-winning poet (1932-1963), also known for her autobiographical novel *The Bell Jar* (1963). Wagner-Martin emphasizes Plath's life as writer, drawing on both published and unpublished writings. The book describes her childhood, her education (including her time at Smith College), her guest-editorship at *Mademoiselle* and subsequent nervous breakdown, her marriage to poet Ted Hughes, her experience of motherhood, and her friendships with other women. Illustrations.

Welty, Eudora. *One Writer's Beginnings*. Cambridge, Mass.: Harvard University Press, 1984.
Memoirs of the short-story writer and novelist (born 1909), concentrating on how her childhood and family in Jackson, Mississippi, shaped her as a writer and dictated her material. The book consists of three long essays describing Welty's "sheltered life" but concludes that such a life can be daring because "all serious daring starts from within." Illustrations.

Wolff, Cynthia Griffin. *Emily Dickinson*. New York: Alfred A. Knopf, 1986.
Critical biography of one of the most important American poets (1830-1886), including readings of many of her deceptively simple poems. Wolff views Dickinson as "an artist of the age of transition," reflecting changes in U.S. society and culture, especially regarding the individual's identity and relation to God. The study emphasizes the social and historical context and Dickinson's family history and presents her as a serious poet (in opposition to the pervasive image of her as a phantom spinster). Illustrations. Index of first lines.

Music

Ammer, Christine. *Unsung: A History of Women in American Music*. Westport, Conn.: Greenwood Press, 1980.
History of American women composers, conductors, and performers, begin-

ning with a brief outline of the Colonial period and continuing through the
twentieth century. Chapters discuss a separate American women's music tradition ("lady violinists," "lady composers," and all-women orchestras) and
women as part of a larger tradition (including opera and women composing in
both European and American idioms). Ammer seeks to redress what she sees
as the ignorance and rejection of women's contributions to mainstream music.
Appendices provide data on National Endowment for the Arts awards to
women. Bibliography.

Balliett, Whitney. *American Singers: Twenty-seven Portraits in Song*. New York:
Oxford University Press, 1988.
Profiles of American jazz singers, including many women. Among the subjects
are Albert Hunter, Peggy Lee, Margaret Whiting, Mabel Mercer, Blossom
Dearie, and Betty Carter. The essays, most of which originally appeared in *The
New Yorker*, combine biography and criticism, draw on extensive interviews
with the singers and their associates, and often include vivid descriptions of
performances.

Bowers, Jane, and Judith Tick, eds. *Women Making Music: The Western Art Tradi-
tion, 1150-1950*. Urbana: University of Illinois Press, 1986.
Essays by musicologists on women musicians. Contributors discuss a wide
range of topics, including nuns and secular French musicians of the Middle
Ages; women singers and songs and professional women musicians of the
Italian Renaissance; individual women composers, including Clara Schumann,
Dame Ethel Smyth, Ruth Crawford Seeger (including Seeger discography); and
women's orchestras from 1925 to 1945. Editors' introduction describes the
book as a corrective of music historians' omission of women, surveys the
history of women in music, and considers the impact of women's status within
the profession on their art. Illustrations, figures, tables.

Cohen, Aaron I. *International Encyclopedia of Women Composers*. New York:
R. R. Bowker, 1981.
Encyclopedia of more than five thousand women composers from around the
world, listing both contemporary figures and women dating back to ancient
Greece. Entries include biographical information, lists of compositions, and an
individual bibliography, where relevant. Classical, sacred, and choral music are
represented. "Notable Facts About Women Composers" presents a list of firsts
and interesting trivia. Appendices include lists by country and century and an
index of women composers about whom too little is known for a full entry.
Illustrations. Bibliography.

Koskoff, Ellen, ed. *Women and Music in Cross-Cultural Perspective*. New York:
Greenwood Press, 1987.

Essays on women and a wide range of music from a variety of cultures. Topics include women in American music—the nineteenth century hymnody tradition, New Orleans jazz, New York Hasidim—and women and music from cultures as diverse as those of Java, Japan, Greece, India, Brazil, and Moroccan Jews living in Canada. Contributors address both vocal and instrumental music, with an emphasis on women as performers and composers, but some attention is also paid to imagery and associations with the feminine. Editor's introduction describes the collection as dealing with the implications of gender for performance within the context of an individual society's gender ideology, reviews ethnomusicologic literature and gender-related issues, and considers music as an agent in inter-gender relations. Essays include Karen E. Peterson's "An Investigation into Women-Identified Music in the United States" and Carol E. Robertson's "Power and Gender in the Musical Experience of Women." Illustrations, mostly excerpts from musical scores.

LePage, Jane Weiner. *Women Composers, Conductors, and Musicians of the Twentieth Century*. 3 vols. Metuchen, N.J.: Scarecrow Press, 1980-1988.
Biographies of women in music, including basics about their lives, excerpts from program notes and other writings on music, and reviews—with partial lists of compositions or recordings where relevant. Essays discuss music, and some consider issues specific to women in music. Selection includes women associated with a range of serious and classical music (Antonia Brico, Wanda Landowska, Sarah Cauldwell), women's music (Kay Gardner), and women simultaneously involved in other arts. Illustrations.

Neuls-Baker, Carol, ed. *Women in Music: An Anthology of Source Readings from the Middle Ages to the Present*. New York: Harper & Row, 1982.
Reprints readings on women in Western art music, especially composers and performers. Includes accounts by women themselves (teachers, performers, and composers) and by contemporary critics, historians. Readings are grouped into historical sections: Middle Ages, Renaissance, Baroque, Classical, 1820-1920, and 1920-1981. Each selection is introduced by a headnote providing historical and other context. Illustrations. Index, bibliography.

Placksin, Sally. *American Women in Jazz, 1900 to the Present: Their Words, Lives, and Music*. New York: Seaview Books, 1982.
A history of women's role in and contribution to jazz, presented in decade-by-decade groups of short biographical essays drawing on interviews with women singers and instrumentalists. The book begins with "Prehistory (1619-1900)," tracing black women's music in America from the arrival of the first woman slave. "The Twenties" includes short essays on singers ("The Blues Women") and instrumentalists. Placksin considers both major and less well-known performers, providing short biographies, critical evaluations, and musical con-

texts—along with discussions of larger trends and male musicians. Illustrations. Selected discography by artist.

Steward, Sue, and Sheryl Garratt. *Signed, Sealed, and Delivered: True Life Stories of Women in Pop*. Boston: South End Press, 1984.
A feminist history of women in rock and pop, from the mid-1950's to the mid-1980's, covering a wide range of music—including soul, rhythm and blues, country, punk, jazz, salsa, reggae, African pop, and rockabilly. Based on interviews with women musicians and singers, the book attempts to correct the omission of women's contributions to rock. (Although the main subject is British women and musical forms, the transatlantic nature of rock music means that many American performers are included.) Includes discussion of women and girls as fans. Illustrations. Reading list and discography.

Taylor, Frank C., with Gerald Cook. *Alberta Hunter: A Celebration in Blues*. New York: McGraw-Hill, 1987.
Biography of the blues singer and songwriter (1895-1984), from her Memphis childhood as the daughter of a black sleeping-car porter, to her entry into the Chicago blues scene, European tours and stage successes, retirement in late 1950's, career as a nurse, and highly publicized 1977 comeback. Includes a consideration of racism and of Hunter's lesbian relationships and provides a vivid picture of the evolution of the blues in the twentieth century. Discography and videography. Illustrations.

Tilchen, Maida. "Lesbians and Women's Music." In *Women-Identified Women*, edited by Trudy Darty and Sandee Potter. Palo Alto, Calif.: Mayfield, 1984.
Traces the development of "women's music" from Maxine Feldman's 1969 "Angry Arthis," the first women's music record released. Tilchen discusses the connections between performance and recording and the lesbian community, including arguments over separatism and the growth of women's music festivals.

Wenner, Hilda E., and Elizabeth Freilicher. *Here's to the Women: One Hundred Songs for and About American Women*. Foreword by Pete Seeger. Syracuse, N.Y.: Syracuse University Press, 1987.
Anthology of folk songs (with music) by and about women, covering all types of folk traditions. Introduction explains selections and describes individual sections. Songs are grouped by theme: friends and lovers, activism, labor, contemporary issues, growing up, role models, and "women emerging." Includes songs by Holly Near, Buffy Sainte-Marie, and Peggy Seeger. Useful discography, lists of songbooks and children's music resources, and a bibliography of catalogs. Annotated references. Index of titles and first lines.

Zaimont, Judith Lang, and Karen Famera, eds. and comps. *Contemporary Concert Music by Women: A Directory of Composers and Their Works*. Westport, Conn.: Greenwood Press, 1981.
Short biographies of women composers and selected musicians involved in the International League of Women Composers. Includes classified list of music by genre and medium, discography, and record company address list. Illustrations, including photographs and some facsimiles of compositions.

Mass Media, Film, and Popular Culture

Bathrick, Serafina. *"The Mary Tyler Moore Show*: Women at Home and at Work." In *MTM: "Quality Television,"* edited by Jane Feuer, Paul Kerr, and Tise Vahimagi. London: British Film Institute, 1984.
A detailed analysis of *The Mary Tyler Moore Show*, concentrating on how the character of Mary Richards is situated in her work and home contexts. Bathrick argues that Mary's work- and home-centered friendships provide a model of a new kind of family group. (The essay also includes discussions of all the major female characters on the series, as well as the male characters' attitudes toward Mary.)

De Lauretis, Teresa. *Alice Doesn't: Feminism, Semiotics, Cinema*. Bloomington: Indiana University Press, 1984.
Extremely influential theoretical feminist analysis of film and film theory, drawing on semiotics, psychoanalysis, and feminist criticism. Chapters consider specific films and filmmaking in general (including women's cinema), issues of narrative and of visual representation, and the contradictions of women's subjectivity. Because of de Lauretis' frequent focus on the theoretical level, the book is often difficult. Includes index of films discussed.

Erens, Patricia, ed. *Sexual Strategems: The World of Women in Film*. New York: Horizon Press, 1979.
Essays on women in film, including representations of women and specific individual directors and films. Grouped into male-directed cinema and women's cinema, essays explore both traditional and alternative cinema. Contributors include Molly Haskell, Claire Johnston, Julia Lesage ("Feminist Film Criticism: Theory and Practice"). Extensive and valuable filmographies of individual women directors. Illustrations. Bibliography.

Fishburn, Katherine. *Women in Popular Culture: A Reference Guide*. Westport, Conn.: Greenwood Press, 1982.
Review essays, all with bibliographies, on all aspects of women in popular culture, defined broadly to include both cultural artifacts and aspects of culture

such as work and politics. Chapters include the history of women in popular literature; magazines and magazine fiction; film; television; advertising, fashion, sports, and comics; and theories of women in popular culture. Introduction presents a historical review of American popular culture, including a discussion of black women and women and art. Fishburn argues that women as a group are used to represent American social mythology. Appendices include lists of selected periodicals, special issues; bibliographies, biographies, and other guides; chronology; and research centers and institutions.

Goffman, Erving. *Gender Advertisements*. New York: Harper & Row, 1979.
Analysis of the representation of gender in advertising, emphasizing the way that advertisements use physical positioning and other methods to present women as childlike, subordinate, and lacking in authority. Goffman argues that, although people recognize commercials as fantasy, the acceptance of these portrayals as realistic carries over into the perceptions of actual gender relations. Includes more than five hundred pictures from print advertisements to illustrate the argument.

Haskell, Molly. *From Reverence to Rape: The Treatment of Women in the Movies*. New York: Holt, Rinehart & Winston, 1974. Rev. ed. Chicago: University of Chicago Press, 1987.
One of the first book-length feminist analyses of women as actresses and film characters. Haskell considers women in film in decade-by-decade chapters, with additional chapters on the "woman's film" of the 1930's and 1940's (usually associated with actresses such as Bette Davis and Joan Crawford) and on European directors. She argues that Hollywood films present an especially compelling version of "the big lie" of women's inferiority and that these presentations contradict the fact that the film industry has actually made individual women—the major actresses—extremely powerful. Haskell particularly targets films (such as the "woman's film") that emphasize the need for women to sacrifice career for love. She also, however, dislikes what she calls "sociological criticism"—that is, criticism based on an exclusively political agenda like feminism—and argues for the importance of knowing about film history and understanding the complex relationship between film and social stereotypes. The revised edition includes a new preface and a chapter on films from 1974 to 1987. Illustrations.

Kaplan, E. Ann. "Feminist Criticism and Television." In *Channels of Discourse: Television and Contemporary Criticism*, edited by Robert C. Allen. Chapel Hill: University of North Carolina Press, 1987.
Overview of recent feminist criticism of television, introducing fairly sophisticated theoretical approaches from a variety of feminist perspectives. Includes a discussion of differences between feminist film and television studies, the

influence of psychoanalytic theory, questions of visual representation of women, and discussions of individual books and essays. The essay concludes with an analysis of Music Television (MTV) as an example of how television represents women and the feminine. Bibliographic essay will guide readers to additional sources.

Kuhn, Annette. *Women's Pictures: Feminism and Cinema*. Boston: Routledge & Kegan Paul, 1982.
Major feminist theoretical analysis of representation of women in film. Using examples from specific films—by both mainstream and avant-garde directors and by women and men—Kuhn describes the means by which film constructs spectators, women, and the feminine, arguing that film is an appropriate and important arena for feminist intervention through criticism and alternative filmmaking. A difficult analysis, assuming familiarity with film theory and feminist critical vocabulary. Appendices provide glossary of film terms and sources for films discussed in text. Illustrations.

Miller, Lynn Feldman. *The Hand That Holds the Camera: Interviews with Women Film and Video Directors*. New York: Garland, 1988.
Interviews with women directors (including Michelle Citron, Linda Yellin, and Doris Chase) about their personal experiences as directors. Miller's questions address issues related to women and film, problems women directors face, and feminism and filmmaking. Her introduction argues that, in contrast to mainstream Hollywood filmmaking, which assumes a male spectator, feminist film practice is characterized by a "woman's gaze," demonstrated through the filmmaker's choice of performers and stories and the degree of intimacy in both fictional and documentary films by women. Each interview is introduced by biographical sketch and includes chronology of films and videos for each director. Illustrations.

Modleski, Tania. *Loving with a Vengeance: Mass-Produced Fantasies for Women*. New York: Methuen, 1984.
Study of popular culture aimed at women (Harlequin romances, gothic novels, and soap operas). Modleski analyzes narrative and other strategies used in these forms. She argues that these genres fulfill women's fantasies about love and family but also provide subtle images of resistance to women's secondary status. (For example, soap opera "villainesses" shape their own fates by manipulating other characters.)

Newland, Kathleen. "Women in Words and Pictures." In her *The Sisterhood of Man*. New York: W. W. Norton, 1979.
General discussion of mass media images of women around the world, emphasizing the power of the media to influence audience attitudes toward stereo-

types and political change. Newland considers news reporting and newspapers, women's magazines, radio, and television, and argues that media bias against women rests on a pervasive tradition of sexism. She believes that women's greater participation in media production would improve content but emphasizes the position of the media within larger social and economic structures. Tables.

Pribram, E. Deidre, ed. *Female Spectators: Looking at Film and Television*. New York: Verso, 1988.
A collection of scholarly essays on film and television, focusing on women as both producers and consumers of films and television programs. Editor's introduction considers the notion of the female spectator, including questions about how feminist critics and theorists have taken up and revised psychoanalytic and semiotic theory. Contributors analyze individual films (*Mildred Pierce, The Color Purple, Rear Window*), women as filmmakers, and how psychoanalytic theory can be used in film and television theory. Includes essays by filmmaker Michelle Citron, theorist Teresa de Lauretis. Selected reading list.

Tuchman, Gaye, Arlene Daniels, and James Benet, eds. *Hearth and Home: Images of Women in the Mass Media*. New York: Oxford University Press, 1978.
Essays on women and television (including effects on children), women's magazines, and women's newspapers (including "women's pages"). Tuchman's introduction describes the "symbolic annihilation" of women by mass media—media representations as symbolic, rather than literal portrayals of women—and the impact of media sex-role stereotypes. She also reviews the three areas of media, the lessons they teach women, and approaches to research. Benet's conclusion argues that only greater control of media by women owners (not simply women executives or managers) will lead to improved images of women. Includes annotated bibliography on images of women on television. Figures and tables.

WOMEN'S ISSUES

INDEX

INDEX

INDEX

INDEX